As one of the world's longest established
and best-known travel brands,
Thomas Cook are the experts in travel.

For more than 135 years our
guidebooks have unlocked the secrets
of destinations around the world,
sharing with travellers a wealth of
experience and a passion for travel.

**Rely on Thomas Cook as your
travelling companion on your next trip
and benefit from our unique heritage.**

Thomas Cook **pocket** guides

KERALA

Your travelling companion since 1873

Thomas
Cook

Written by Debbie Stowe.
Original photography by Vasile Szakacs

Published by Thomas Cook Publishing
A division of Thomas Cook Tour Operations Limited
Company registration no. 3772199 England
The Thomas Cook Business Park, Unit 9, Coningsby Road,
Peterborough PE3 8SB, United Kingdom
Email: books@thomascook.com, Tel: + 44 (0) 1733 416477
www.thomascookpublishing.com

Produced by Cambridge Publishing Management Limited
Burr Elm Court, Main Street, Caldecote CB23 7NU
www.cambridgepm.co.uk

ISBN: 978-1-84848-258-6

First edition © 2010 Thomas Cook Publishing
Text © Thomas Cook Publishing
Maps © Thomas Cook Publishing/PCGraphics (UK) Limited

Project Editor: Adam Royal
Production/DTP: Steven Collins

Printed and bound in Spain by GraphyCems

Cover photography © Felix Hug, Getty Images

CONTENTS

WHAT'S IN YOUR GUIDEBOOK?

Independent authors Impartial, up-to-date information from our travel experts who meticulously source local knowledge.

Experience Thomas Cook's 165 years in the travel industry and guidebook publishing enrich every word with expertise you can trust.

Travel know-how Thomas Cook has thousands of staff working around the globe, all living and breathing travel.

Editors Travel-publishing professionals, pulling everything together to craft a perfect blend of words, pictures, maps and design.

You, the traveller We deliver a practical, no-nonsense approach to information, geared to how you really use it.

ABOUT THE AUTHOR

Debbie Stowe is a freelance journalist, travel writer and author. She has written over a dozen non-fiction and travel books, specialising in Indian Ocean and Eastern European destinations. Her writing also covers the natural world, film, human rights and cultural and social issues. She lives in Bucharest with her partner.

❍ *Boats are a useful means of transport in aquatically orientated Kochi*

INTRODUCTION
Getting to know Kerala

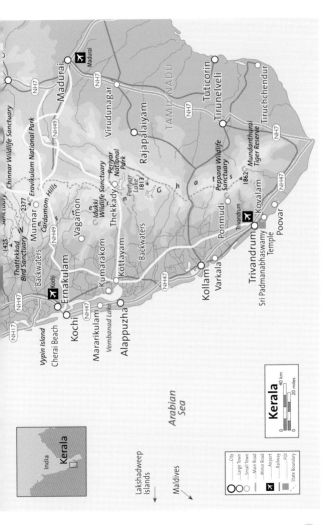

Getting to know Kerala

With palm-fringed beaches, awe-inspiring mountains, dreamy backwaters, a vibrant cultural scene and all the chaotic charm that India is known for, Kerala is pretty much a country within a country. Spend any time here among its lush greenery and friendly, open people and the state tourist board's appropriation of the famous New Zealand slogan 'God's own country' becomes perfectly understandable.

Nestled down in the southwest corner of India, Kerala is a long, thin state that runs along the Malabar Coast. Its western side borders the shimmering Arabian Sea; its eastern edge is part of the Western Ghats, a biodiversity bonanza of a mountain range. There's certainly tough competition for the accolade, but Kerala's most impressive geographical asset is probably its backwaters, a mystical network of lagoons, lakes, islands and villages that justifiably tops many visitors' must-see list. A few days spent cruising this aquatic labyrinth offers an enchanting glimpse into a different world.

There's also something a bit other-worldly about Keralan culture. Best summed up by its *kathakali* dance-dramas – melodramatic supernatural tales performed by the most fabulously made-up actors you will ever see – it's a vivid picture of a state that is proud of its history and traditions.

Keralans are also fiercely proud of their education system. The highest literacy and lowest corruption rates in India coupled with a good healthcare system mean that the state is not as blighted by poverty as much of the rest of the country. Women also enjoy a relatively good time of it here. The decent standards of living are visible in the contentment of the people, and you'd be hard pushed to find a destination where you are extended such a warm welcome. From excited schoolchildren jostling to shake your hand to the amiable waves from other holidaymakers and denizens of the backwaters as you sail serenely by, Keralan cordiality and curiosity will be among your lasting memories of this special state. Still a relative newcomer to the tourist map, it lacks the hard sell of, say, Goa, and it's easy to get off the beaten track if you want to.

⬥ *The lush greenery of Kerala in its full glory at Eravikulam National Park*

But while it often feels self-contained, Kerala is still teeming with everything that makes India such an intoxicating destination. Dazzling temples, astonishing architecture, delightful wildlife, towns and villages that are a whirl of colour and noise, zesty food and soothing Ayurveda massages all ensure that your Keralan adventure will be much more than just a brilliant beach holiday.

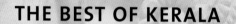

THE BEST OF KERALA

Kerala's incredible diversity allows you to pack an enormous amount into a short time, whether it's history, culture, beach fun, food or R&R that floats your boat.

TOP 10 ATTRACTIONS

- **Take an authentic course of Ayurveda treatment** or just an indulgent one-off massage (see pages 35 & 104).

- **Mess about in boats on Kerala's backwaters** – Kerala's exotically tranquil waterways make it the Venice of the East (see pages 76–8).

- **Revisit the days of the Raj** with a stay in Munnar's beautifully preserved scenic hill station (see pages 81–2).

- **Stray off the beaten track and flop down on Muzhappilangad Beach**, one of the prettiest in Kerala (see pages 60–1).

- **Visit quirky Kochi** and check out the Chinese fishing nets, slew of striking buildings and sophisticated restaurant scene (see pages 41–52).

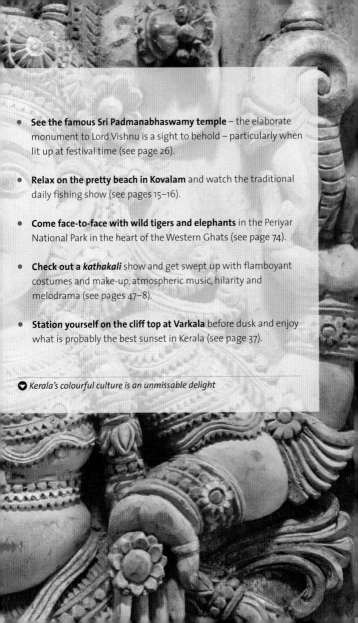

- **See the famous Sri Padmanabhaswamy temple** – the elaborate monument to Lord Vishnu is a sight to behold – particularly when lit up at festival time (see page 26).

- **Relax on the pretty beach in Kovalam** and watch the traditional daily fishing show (see pages 15–16).

- **Come face-to-face with wild tigers and elephants** in the Periyar National Park in the heart of the Western Ghats (see page 74).

- **Check out a *kathakali* show** and get swept up with flamboyant costumes and make-up, atmospheric music, hilarity and melodrama (see pages 47–8).

- **Station yourself on the cliff top at Varkala** before dusk and enjoy what is probably the best sunset in Kerala (see page 37).

◆ *Kerala's colourful culture is an unmissable delight*

SYMBOLS KEY

The following symbols are used throughout this book:

ⓐ address ☎ telephone ⓦ website address ⓔ email ⓕ fax

ⓛ opening times ⓘ important ⓝ public transport

The following symbols are used on the maps:

𝒊	information office	○	city
✉	post office	○	large town
🛍	shopping	○	small town
✈	airport	■	POI (point of interest)
✚	hospital	—	main road
♺	police station	—	minor road
🚍	bus station	—	railway
🚆	railway station		
✝	cathedral		
❶	numbers denote featured cafés, restaurants & evening venues		

RESTAURANT CATEGORIES

The symbol after the name of each restaurant listed in the guide indicates the price of a typical three-course meal without drinks for one person.

£ = up to Rs 300   ££ = Rs 300–600   £££ = over Rs 600

▶ *Kochi's quirky Chinese fishing nets are a distinctively Keralan sight*

RESORTS
Places under the sun

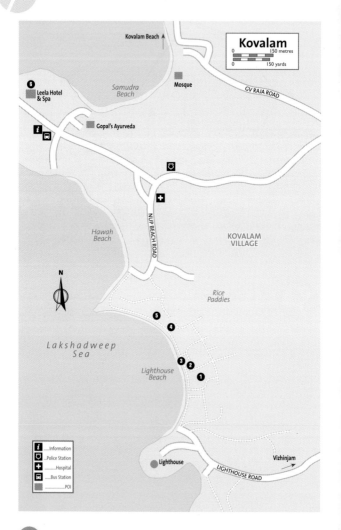

Kovalam Beach ↑

Kovalam
0 — 150 metres
0 — 150 yards

Samudra Beach

Mosque

GV RAJA ROAD

Leela Hotel & Spa

Gopal's Ayurveda

NUP BEACH ROAD

Hawah Beach

KOVALAM VILLAGE

N

Lakshadweep Sea

Rice Paddies

Lighthouse Beach

Lighthouse

Vizhinjam →

LIGHTHOUSE ROAD

i .... Information
🔯 .... Police Station
✚ .... Hospital
🚌 .... Bus Station
⬛ .... POI

Kovalam

Kovalam's reputation as some sort of overdeveloped Costa del Kerala is exaggerated, and the resort has a low-key charm that makes it a nice little spot to kick back and enjoy the traditional pleasures of the beach. Admittedly, it's no longer the quiet fishing village that it once was, but vestiges of that time remain, and the daily ritual of the morning catch is still going strong. The fact that it is still a working village gives Kovalam its character and separates it from the more touristy resorts on India's west coast, such as Baga and Calangute in Goa.

Hotels, eateries and shops line Kovalam's coastline, and the promenade (which might be too grand a word for the ramshackle strip of concrete that runs along the beach) has a pleasant bustle to it, thronging in high season with visitors and hawkers. But everything happens in an enjoyably unpretentious way. The narrow network of pathways that connect the beach area with much of the accommodation a little further back are muddy and unlit, and ambling along them with your torch you certainly won't feel like you're in a nightmare of overdevelopment and commercialism.

Aside from sand-based activities, there's not a whole lot to actually do in the resort. Kovalam is more about enjoying the laid-back Indian beach vibe and eating, drinking and shopping in an exotic location while having all the amenities you need at hand. One positive side of the town's 'commercialisation' is that if you want to spend western cash, top quality accommodation and meals are on hand. If you really take exception to a touristy ambience, just try to schedule your trip slightly outside peak season, when more of Kovalam's tradition as a simple fishing village is evident to the visitor.

BEACHES

Whether you like your beach lively or lonely, there's a stretch of sand in Kovalam to suit. The resort's southernmost one is called **Lighthouse Beach** – for obvious reasons: the 35 m (115 ft)-high construction on top of

Kurumkal hillock. It is this crescent-shaped beach that attracts the most tourists, probably because of its aesthetic appeal, but it also boasts the most facilities. The cove is not entirely given over to leisure and recreation; you will still see fishermen hauling that night's dinner out of the sea – one of Kovalam's more picturesque images. Lifeguards operate here – and with good reason; tides can result in dangerous currents, so take care when swimming.

Moving northwards, the next cove is **Hawah** (sometimes Hawa) **Beach**, which sits a rocky outcrop away from Lighthouse. Its name is said to come from the topless women who used to sunbathe there, and the place was reputedly India's first topless beach. The practice is now banned, apart from where the coastline is privately owned by a hotel. But the lack of flesh on display now doesn't seem to have dented Hawah's allure, and it can still get fairly crowded in high season.

⬥ *Traditions live on in Kovalam's fishing community*

Keep going north, over the hill, to get to **Samudra Beach**, cut off from the rest of the shoreline by headland. If you're after sand-based solitude, it's worth the trek. Secluded and serene, the few people you find here are more likely to be catching fish than rays. It's here to the north – and also to the south of the lighthouse – that coastal India 'proper' can be found, although some of it has been designated private beach for a hotel. The hardcore 'getting away from it all' brigade could also head 2 km (1¼ miles) south of Kovalam to the workaday port of **Vizhinjam**, famous for its rock-cut temple and sculptures. Throughout the area the sand can be black in parts, owing to its mineral make-up.

THINGS TO SEE & DO

Gopal's Ayurveda

Kovalam does not present the visitor with a long list of compelling sights and attractions, but in Kerala it's usually possible to indulge in some Ayurveda treatments. Indulge is perhaps not the right word at Gopal's, where it's all about Ayurvedic authenticity rather than massage luxury, but you can't argue with the bargain prices when a massage doesn't set you back much more than a curry and a beer. Longer courses of treatments spanning several days are also available.

ⓐ Samudra Beach ⓣ (0471) 248 0833 ⓦ www.sarisafari.com/gopals
ⓔ gopalsayurva@yahoo.co.in ⓛ 08.00–17.00 daily

TAKING A BREAK

Suprabhatham £ ❶ Serves cheap-as-chips veggie eats that are so good even committed carnivores will be won over. Service is warm and welcoming, and the inviting, palm-dense environs make up for the absence of the sound of gently lapping waves. The cuisine is old-school Keralan. ⓐ 200 m (650 ft) from Lighthouse Beach; take the path between German Bakery and Waves and the Hotel Orion
ⓛ 07.00–23.00 daily

German Bakery and Waves ££ ❷ One of the few eateries on Kovalam's main drag to look trendy and professional, the German Bakery and Waves are firm favourites on the scene. Great during the day, when you can feast on scrumptious pastries, quiche, strudel and fresh bread, this popular haunt also churns out first-rate fare from Thai to tofu, not forgetting the ubiquitous seafood and pasta. ❸ Lighthouse Beach ❶ (0471) 248 0179 ❷ 07.00–23.00 daily

Volga ££ ❸ A rooftop location and helpful staff are the highlights of this beachside eatery, where seafood (of course), Indian, Chinese and continental fare is consumed from atop green checked tablecloths. ❸ Lighthouse Beach ❶ (0471) 248 3286 ❷ 07.00–23.00 daily

AFTER DARK

Kovalam's coastal location and active fishing industry make its tasty seafood a must-try. Restaurants along the resort's main drag, the promenade alongside Lighthouse Beach, compete for customers by displaying fresh fish outside their premises. They also station staff members outside, keen to tempt potential diners in.

Beatles Food & Music Club ££ ❹ Liverpool might be a long way from Kovalam, but it doesn't feel like it here. To the occasional strains of live music – and, if not, good recorded tunes – this well reputed and amiable Fab Four-themed place serves up delicious seafood, hauled from the sea just metres away that morning. You can also enjoy your pick of Indian, European and even Himalayan staples while looking out over the sea. A tempting selection of cakes is also on display. ❸ Lighthouse Beach ❷ 08.00–23.00 daily

Fusion ££ ❺ A cool and creative first-floor restaurant that plays with different cuisines (as the name suggests) to give a different take on the old staples. If you're not in an adventurous mood, stick to jacket potato, pizza or curry. Round things off with one of their fine teas or coffees –

◢ *Palm trees overlooking Kovalam beach*

◐ *A vendor transports her wares on her head in the time-honoured way*

or something stronger, as they serve alcohol. The trendy design and lively atmosphere have won Fusion legions of fans. ⓐ Lighthouse Beach ⓣ (0471) 248 1243 ⓔ fusion_in_kovalam@yahoo.co.in ⓛ 07.00–23.00 daily

The Tides £££ ⓰   For the best of fine dining in Kovalam, the only real choice is the Leela Hotel. Wicker chairs and glass-topped tables set off with tastefully crossed white table drapes and candles ooze class. The high-end victuals are Pan-Asian and – as you'd expect in a beachside restaurant – include a large seafood selection. The hotel has several other posh restaurants worthy of your time and taste buds. ⓐ Leela Hotel, north of Hawah Beach ⓣ 934 992 2426 ⓛ 11.00–23.00 daily

DRINKING IN KERALA

Most of the smaller Kovalam restaurants don't serve alcohol – at least officially – as the cost of an alcohol licence makes it prohibitive for small businesses. Some use ingenious ways to subvert the restriction. Beer, spirits and so on will not be listed on the menu. When they come, they may be served in opaque mugs, preventing any passing officials from seeing what colour liquid is being imbibed. Bottles are sometimes served in bags, and drinkers asked to keep their tipple under the table. A minimum of alcohol will be kept on the premises so it can be claimed it's for personal use only. Of course, you may be unlucky and pitch up in a restaurant that actually respects the rules!

RESORTS

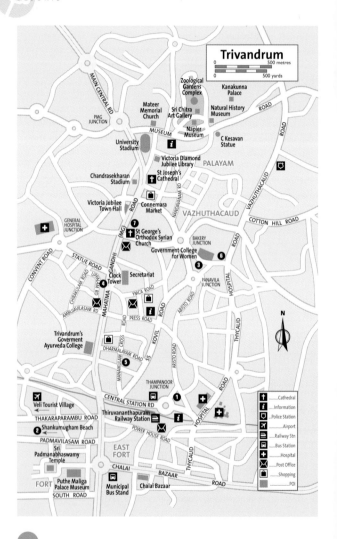

Trivandrum

The multi-syllabic mouthful that is the state capital's original name, Thiruvananthapuram, explains why many people still refer to it by its British moniker – Trivandrum. A gateway to Kerala thanks to its airport, many travellers pass quickly through Trivandrum on their way to the more popular beach resorts of Varkala to the north and Kovalam to the south, but it has enough going for it to merit a brief sojourn.

As capitals go, it is agreeably small and manageable, with most of the highlights clustered fairly closely together. It's also less frenetic than most urban metropolises, and passengers touching down at its airport from out of state or overseas will find it refreshingly lush and verdant, its tropical humidity signalling a more relaxed way of carrying on than in dryer climes. The laid-back living can also make Trivandrum a preferable base for those who find tourist hotspot Kovalam a little too bustling.

Another reason to linger a while in Trivandrum before hitting the beach is its wealth of cultural attractions, the flagship one being the Sri Padmanabhaswamy Temple. And the town has a historical charm, exemplified by the remainder of a fort wall, the vestiges of royal Thiruvananthapuram. A humbler side of traditional Kerala is also on view, in the serpentine city back streets with their old-world commerce. Things centre on the Mahatma Ghandi Road (known locally as MG Road), from which the main highlights are either walkable or a short rickshaw hop away.

BEACHES

Trivandrum's sands tend to get overlooked as sun-seekers hotfoot it to either Kovalam or Varkala, but if you're going to be based in the town for any period you can get in some beach time. Clean, wide, calm and sandy, **Shankumugham Beach** lies to the west of the city, not far from the airport. There's a surprising amount of things to do here, including a roller-skating rink (lessons are available), indoor sports complex offering badminton and table tennis and a few refreshments outlets (one of which is shaped like a starfish). Beachgoers can even have their fill of culture: Shankumugham's most eye-catching feature is Jalakanyaka, a 35 m (115 ft)-long statue of a reclining mermaid by the highly rated local sculptor Kanayi Kunhiraman. Another monument is the stone pavilion. Children will find plenty to entertain them at the Jawaharlal Nehru Park, while newly built walkways provide a nice spot for an evening promenade.

If you like your beach experience to be more landscaped, another option is the **Veli Tourist Village**, a tourist-orientated park developed between Veli lagoon and the Arabian Sea. A thin sandbar separates the large boating lake from the sea, and there are also watersports, picnic and restaurant facilities, and you can admire the large modern artwork of Kanayi Kunhiraman (again), who is responsible for the enormous – and, it must be said, rather polarising – concrete sculptures.

Veli Tourist Village ⓐ 8 km (5 miles) west of Trivandrum ⓣ (0471) 250 0785 ⓛ 08.00–19.00 daily Ⓝ KSRTC bus no 155 ⓘ Admission charge

ⓐ *Picking up some fragrant flower garlands in Trivandrum*

THINGS TO SEE & DO

Trivandrum's Government Ayurveda College

To sample the massages and treatments of India's traditional healing system without paying high-end hotel prices, pop along to this local Ayurveda training school. You may have to wait, and the venue is on the no-frills side, but the treatment and prior consultation are free, performed by students of the institution.

ⓐ MG Road ❶ (0471) 246 0190 🕙 08.00–13.00 daily

Chalai Bazaar

Trivandrum's long-established retail zone consists of the 2-km (1¼-mile) road of the same name, which runs from east to west, and the series of narrow lanes that branch off it. In the time-honoured style of Indian markets, the key word when describing the shops is eclecticism. Fruit and vegetables are the main game at this frenetic bazaar, but the profusion of small stalls stock anything and everything from silver to saris, furniture to fish and cutlery to coconuts.

ⓐ Chalai Bazaar Road 🕙 Most shops open 09.00–20.00 Mon–Sat, closed Sun Ⓝ The municipal bus stand, from where you can get to Kovalam, is north of Ghandi Park

Puthe Maliga Palace Museum

This 200-year-old royal residence is the fruit of five years of labour by some 5,000 workers. Today the blue bloods are long gone and their aristo-artefacts form the bulk of the museum. Exquisite thrones, an ivory cradle, portraits of the maharajas, a mini arsenal of weapons and glass imported from Belgium hint at how the other half lived. Some exhibits cover the area's colourful involvement in the spice trade. The palace, with its serene gardens and carved wooden ceiling, is an attraction in its own right.

ⓐ Fort area, south of the tank 🕙 08.30–13.00 & 15.00–17.00 Tues–Sun, closed Mon ❶ Admission charge; shoes must be removed; your guide will appreciate a tip

Sri Padmanabhaswamy Temple

Trivandrum's iconic building is this sprawling temple complex, more than 250 years old, which gave the city its name (the long one). Sadly for tourists, it's not open to non-Hindus. But the fantastic views from the outside alone merit a visit. Make sure to follow the path round to the right of the gate to enjoy the temple to its best effect. If you happen to see it when it is lit up at festival time, the sight is breathtaking. Dominating the scene is the building's seven-tiered *gopuram* (the monumental tower at the temple entrance), which rises 30 m (100 ft) into the air. In a staggering logistical feat, the temple's deity is said to be made up of more than 12,000 sacred stones that were transported by elephant from Nepal. The shops and small businesses that line the temple's distinctive approach road can round off the visit.

ⓐ Inside the fort ❶ (0471) 245 0233 ❗ Closed to non-Hindus

Zoological Gardens Complex

If your time in Trivandrum is short and you want to make the best use of it you can, swing by the Zoological Gardens Complex, a self-contained area with four attractions in one. The biggie is the **Zoological Gardens** – 22 hectares (55 acres) of land that is home to 75 species of wildlife, including endangered indigenous creatures such as the lion-tailed macaque, Nilgiri tahr, Indian rhino, Asiatic lion and Royal Bengal tiger, as well as interlopers from Africa such as giraffes, hippos and zebras. If your trip isn't taking you to Periyar or one of the other wildlife hubs this is a good substitute. Flora fans will also enjoy the abundance of plant life.

If all these animals have piqued your interest, step into the **Natural History Museum**, in the southeast corner of the site. The models and stuffed animals might seem a little musty and old-fashioned to visitors

> **COMBINING TICKETS**
> Though you can pay separately on the door, if you're planning on seeing all of the attractions, you can pick up a combined ticket from the booth near the zoo entrance.

◆ *Sri Padmanabhaswamy Temple is one of Kerala's most iconic religious sites*

⬤ *Easy, tiger: an animal exhibit in the old-school Natural History Museum*

used to newfangled, interactive Western museums, but the collection of skeletons and somewhat ghoulish-looking preserved embryos will grab your attention, and the English captions will help you get a hold (metaphorically) of the fascinating local wildlife. There's also an ethnological gallery with costumes, pictures and models of ships.

First established by the Maharaja of Travancore in 1855, the **Napier Museum** is one of India's oldest. It's been in its present home, an attractive, typically Keralan construction (check out the Gothic roof and minarets), for 130 years. The diverse exhibits, some of which date back over a millennium, run the gamut from sculptures, carvings, idols, handicrafts and instruments to religious paraphernalia (both Hindu and Buddhist).

Round off your visit with a peek inside the **Sri Chitra Art Gallery**, one large room of mostly bright, modernist style paintings, although you will find older works among the predominantly Indian creations on display.
🅐 Museum Road, Palayam ⓦ www.keralamuseumandzoo.org
Zoological gardens 🕒 09.00–18.15 Tues–Sun, closed Mon
❶ Admission charge
Natural History Museum 🕒 10.00–16.45 Tues & Thur–Sun, 13.00–16.45 Wed, closed Mon ❶ Admission charge
Napier Museum 🕒 10.00–16.45 Tues & Thur–Sun, 13.00–16.45 Wed, closed Mon ❶ Admission charge
Sri Chitra Art Gallery 🕒 10.00–16.45 Tues & Thur–Sun, 13.00–16.45 Wed, closed Mon ❶ Admission charge

TAKING A BREAK

Arya Niwas £ ❶ Clean, popular and convenient if you're catching a train, this *thali* (or 'meals') all-you-can-eat outlet serves fresh and tasty traditional fare. It can get busy and trying to customise your order Western style is a no-no but the service is quick. 🅐 Aristo Junction, opposite the railway station ❶ (0471) 233 0789 🕒 07.00–21.00 daily

Indian Coffee House £ ❷ One of almost 400 branches of the workers' collective Indian Coffee House (see box on page 30), this outlet is as interesting from a cultural point of view as it is for a bite to eat. Enjoy your choice of South Indian snacks washed down with coffee or tea while watching the sun set over the sea. Other outlets can be found opposite the zoo and on Central Station Road. ❸ Shankumugham Beach ❶ (0471) 250 5779 🕓 07.30–21.00 daily

Coffee Beanz ££ ❸ Local branch of the hip student hang-out. The coffees are good – as the name would imply – and there's also a decent selection of Western-style snacks such as sandwiches and chips. ❷ Magnet Building, Thycaud, opposite the women's college ❶ (0471) 232 3301 🕓 11.00–22.00 Mon–Sat, 09.00–22.00 Sun

AFTER DARK

Arul Jyothi £ ❹ This centrally located 'meals' restaurant serves up high-quality, low-cost vegetarian staples from both North and South India. It's clean, air-conditioned and the service is friendly. Wash your meal down with a delicious juice. ❸ Opposite the Secretariat, MG Road ❶ (0471) 247 0240; (0471) 247 8497

INDIAN COFFEE HOUSE

Said to be the largest workers' cooperative in the world, the Indian Coffee House chain was first established in the 1940s, in the last years of the British Raj. After more than a decade of operations, it was closed by its founder, the Coffee Board, owing to a change in policy. But rather than docilely accept their fate, the laid-off workers – mobilised by a local communist leader – instead put their money into taking over the branches and began to run them by themselves, setting up cooperative societies. The chain rapidly spread to other parts of India and in 2008 celebrated 50 years of existence.
Ⓦ www.indiancoffeehouse.com

○ *Trivandrum's bustling railway station*

Daavat £ ❺ This pleasantly decorated restaurant at Hotel Regency, with wooden furniture and cheerful yellow walls, serves up Indian, Chinese, European and regional food. It's just 500 m (⅓ mile) from the station, the service is quick and they serve beer. On balmy evenings try Bageecha, the roof garden. ⓐ Manjalikulam Cross Road, Thampanoor ⓣ (0471) 233 0377 ⓦ www.hotelregency.com ⓛ 07.00–23.00 daily

Casa Bianca ££ ❻ If the spices are getting too much for you and you're missing a taste of home, head straight for this Swedish-run pizzeria, restaurant, café, cake and bread shop (which does in fact serve Indian food too). Warm, bright and welcoming, the design, food and ambience all win plaudits. ⓐ 96 MP Appan Road, Vazhuthacaud, opposite Heera Park ⓣ (0471) 233 8323 ⓦ www.casabiancatrivandrum.com ⓛ 12.00–22.00 Tues–Sun, closed Mon

Regency Restaurant ££ ❼ Cut-above-the-rest red-brick hotel restaurant (the name hints at its aspirations) which dishes up Indian, Chinese and continental fare buffet style to the strains of a live band. The hotel also has a (sort of) British-style pub, round-the-clock coffee shop and rooftop barbecue grill. ⓐ The South Park, MG Road ⓣ (0471) 233 3333 ⓦ www.thesouthpark.com ⓛ 12.30–15.00 & 19.30–23.00 daily

Varkala

Along with Kovalam, Varkala is one of Kerala's most famous beach resorts. But while the two are often paired, Varkala, with its thatched roofs and rough greenery, has a markedly different vibe from its more commercial cousin. More relaxed and less in-your-face, this chilled-out beach town attracts the alternative and backpacker crowds, the type of person who deplores too much 'development' and for whom authenticity is the buzzword. In high season you won't be able to walk far in Varkala without hearing the voice of Bob Marley emanating from a nearby beach shack.

What the two resorts do share are their aesthetic charms. At Varkala, the pretty picture is increased by the dramatic cliffs, which are a great place to go to watch the sunset. They are all the more remarkable for being the lone high point in the otherwise flat Keralan coast, and it is this feature that is responsible for a lot of the resort's singularity. The azure waters of the Arabian Sea and army of palms lining the coast complete the idyllic scene.

BEACHES

For now, Varkala's beaches are still less crowded than their Kovalam equivalents. You reach the town's chief stretch of shoreline either by taking the aptly named Beach Road, or, if you're feeling intrepid, the precipitous stairs hewn out of the north cliff face. The coastline between the north and south cliffs is known as **Papanasam Beach**, and it is this part that is the busiest. Its waters are believed to have holy properties, washing away a person's sins. For this reason the area once played host to *vavu beli* (sometimes *vavu bali*), a Hindu custom where believers enter water bearing a concoction of grass, herbs, rice and banana leaf and leave it there to assist the souls of their departed relatives in the afterlife. A big Ayurveda industry has also sprung up here. Today, tourists share the beach with local people. For a touch more seclusion, try **Black Beach**, to the north. As in Kovalam, mineral composition makes the sand dark in some places.

RESORTS

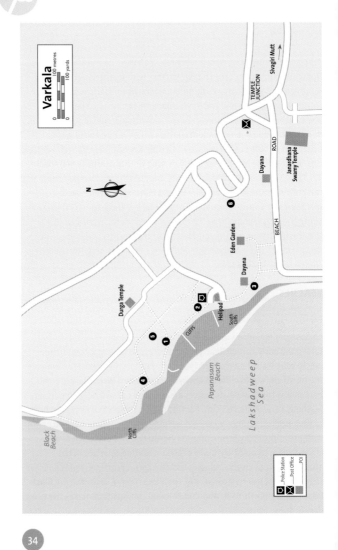

Varkala

0   100 metres
0   100 yards

N

Durga Temple

Black
Beach

North
Cliffs

Papanasam
Beach

CLIFFS

5
1
4

2
Helipad

South
Cliffs

Eden Garden

Dayana

3

6

Dayana

Lakshadweep
Sea

TEMPLE
JUNCTION

Sivagiri Mutt

BEACH   ROAD

Janardhana
Swamy Temple

Police Station
Post Office   POI

Although Varkalans are by now used to Western tourists and their more free-thinking ways, and bikinis are not a rarity, the town is still part of conservative Kerala, and women in swimsuits may attract the unwanted attention of local men. If you're planning a dip, be warned that the waters can sometimes get rough and strong currents can swell up, endangering even competent swimmers. You will normally find lifeguards, and flags indicate the safe perimeter for swimming, but it's unwise to head out too far. The same advice applies if you rent one of the boogie boards on hire from numerous beach outlets.

THINGS TO SEE & DO

Ayurveda

Varkala is something of a hotspot for India's traditional health system, and the resort is teeming with people offering services and products of an Ayurvedic bent. The quality can vary substantially. Reputable providers include **Dayana**, which offers Ayurvedic beauty treatments to women in two outlets, one on the beach itself and the other on Beach Road. The **Eden Garden** resort is another serious and professional operation, providing various treatments from one-offs to lengthier courses, and explaining all the science behind it. Many guesthouses also hold yoga classes.

Dayana ⓐ Papanasam Beach/Beach Road ⓣ (0470) 260 9764; 938 726 1619 ⓔ dayanabeautyclinic@yahoo.com ⓛ 09.00–19.00 daily

Eden Garden ⓐ Papanasam Beach ⓣ (0470) 260 3910 ⓦ www.edengarden.in ⓔ edengarden2000@hotmail.com ⓛ 08.00–18.00 daily

Janardhana Swamy Temple

Bright, bold colours – even by vibrant Hindu standards – make this the resort's flagship building. Thought to be in the region of two millennia old, the temple houses an antediluvian bell that was salvaged from a 17th-century Dutch shipwreck, and subsequently donated by the captain in return for his prayers being answered in the form of no loss of life. Like

RESORTS

many of Kerala's most sacred sites, non-Hindus are not permitted to enter the temple itself but it is sometimes possible to explore the grounds, and in any case the exterior alone repays a visit.

ⓐ NH 47, close to Papanasam Beach ⓛ 05.00–20.00 daily

Sivagiri Mutt

Not exactly a conventional tourist attraction, this place is a Hindu monastery and pilgrimage site. Hardcore types wanting to delve deep and really 'get' India can drop by for a chat with the spiritual master, or swami.

ⓐ 1 km (²/₃ mile) east of town ⓣ (0470) 260 2807 ⓦ www.sivagiri.org
ⓔ mail@sivagiri.org

● *Laid-back Varkala is popular with backpackers and hippies*

Sunset on Varkala's cliffs
It may be something of a cliché, but ascending the cliffs at Varkala shortly before 18.00 and sitting there watching the sun go down will provide you with a romantic holiday memory to savour – and some impressive photographs.

TAKING A BREAK

Varkala's eateries tend to be all-day affairs, opening for breakfast around 08.00 and closing around 23.00.

Juice Shack ££ ❶   Stock up on your vitamin C with a quixotically named fruit blend at this bright and cheery Varkala institution, that also serves a range of healthy and tempting snacks. The internet access is another big draw. ⓐ Behind the Tibetan market ❶ 944 672 8488 ⓔ juiceshack@gmail.com

Oottupura Vegetarian Restaurant ££ ❷   This vegetarian restaurant has a range of local food for all times of the day. If you arrive early, sample the breakfast *puttu*, a rice flour-based dish that comes with milk, fruit and honey. In keeping with the ascetic ethos no alcohol is served. ⓐ By the helipad ❶ (0470) 260 6944

AFTER DARK

Somatheeram £ ❸   Slap bang on the main beach, this no-frills open-air joint has friendly, personal service and high-quality, mainly Indian nourishment. Try the fish in coconut sauce. ⓐ Papanasam Beach

Funky Art Café ££ ❹   Consistently busy, the thatched Funky Art Café pitches itself as the most happening place in town. This is about the nearest you'll get to party action in Kerala, with live shows and music often continuing (relatively) late into the night. Menu highlights include lobster, calamari and steamed fish in banana leaf. The lassis also get rave

◯ A colourful market stall in Varkala

reviews and the chefs even have a stab at Mexican food. Perhaps because of its party vibe, things can get edgy, and women should keep a close eye on their drinks. ⓐ North Cliff

Shiva Garden ££ ❺ Traditional *thali* restaurant serving a classic range of vegetarian and non-vegetarian Keralan fare from which you can savour the views from the red cliffs. Foodies can consult the restaurant's website for a fuller explanation of the local cuisine and menu.
ⓐ North Cliff, Kurakkanni ❶ 934 946 0261 ⓦ www.varkalahomestay.com
ⓔ jayan@varkalahomestay.com ❶ 08.00–11.00, 13.00–15.00 &
18.30–21.30 daily

Cape Comorin £££ ❻ If you've tired of Varkala's backpacker vibe and find yourself yearning for something a little more upmarket, head for the trusty restaurant in the Gateway Hotel. In its former incarnation as Taj Garden Retreat, the Sunday lunch buffet was a big hit. Expect more of the same posh nosh – Indian and international – now it's been redone and renamed. ⓐ Gateway Hotel, Janardhanapuram, near Government Guest House ❶ (0470) 260 3000 ❶ 07.00–23.00

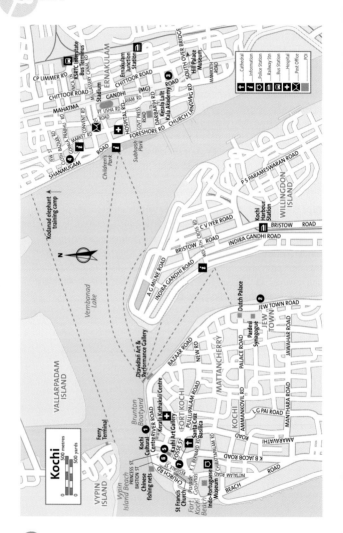

Kochi

0 — 500 metres
0 — 500 yards

VYPIN ISLAND

VALLARPADAM ISLAND

Vembanad Lake

Kodanad elephant training camp

Ferry Terminal

Brunton Boatyard

Dravidian Art & Performance Gallery

Vypin Island Beach

Chinese fishing nets

Kochi Cultural Centre 1

Kashi Art Gallery

Kerala Kathakali Centre

Santa Cruz Basilica

St Francis Church

Fort Kochi Beach

Parade Grounds

Indo-Portuguese Museum

FORT KOCHI

MATTANCHERRY

Dutch Palace

Pardesi Synagogue

JEW TOWN 2

KOCHI

BASTION ST
PRINCESS ST
CHURCH RD
ROSE ST
BURGER ST
QUIROS ST
LILY ST
RIVER RD
HOSPITAL RD
PETER CELLI ST
BERNARD RD
CHIRATTAPALAM RD
PATTALAM ROAD
BEACH
K B JACOB ROAD
AMRAVATHI ROAD
AMMANKOVIL RD
L G PAI ROAD
MANTHARA ROAD
JAWAHAR ROAD
PALACE ROAD
JEW TOWN ROAD
NEW RD
BAZAAR ROAD

WILLINGDON ISLAND

P S PARAMESWARAN ROAD

BRISTOW ROAD

INDIRA GANDHI ROAD

C V IYER ROAD

Harbour Station

WIDTH CROSS RD

A G MILNE ROAD

INDIRA GANDHI ROAD

ERNAKULAM

CP UMMER RD
KSRTC Interstate Bus Terminus
Ernakulam Junction Station

CHITTOOR ROAD
CHITTOOR ROAD

MAHATMA GANDHI (MG) ROAD

JEW ST
CLOTH BAZAAR RD
GOPALA PRABHU RD
MARKET RD
CONVENT RD
PT USHA RD
TG ROAD
AYAM RD
GOVT PRESS ROAD
DARBAR HR RD
CHURCH LANDING RD
HOSPITAL RD
FORESHORE RD

SHANMUGAM ROAD

Stadium

Kerala Lalit Kala Akademi 3

South Over Bridge

Hill Palace Museum

MANIKATH ROAD

Subhash Park

Children's Park

N

Kochi

Kochi is Kerala's most cosmopolitan town by a long way; a stay here is a must for anyone who wants to get the most out of the state's cultural and gastronomic offerings. Despite not being the largest or most populous city, vibrant Kochi certainly feels like this is where the action is. Whether it's the history, shopping, sightseeing or food that you're here for, the city delivers.

In fact, that should be 'cities'. The conurbation formerly known as Kochi is made up of two separate towns, Kochi and Ernakulam. The reason for this rather odd situation is the topography: underwater Malabar mud banks divided the place aquatically, resulting in a natural harbour. Most cross-town journeys involve a leg by ferry, which adds to the leisurely ambience. Perhaps as a consequence of being bisected by glorious blue waters, the two towns feel relatively free of the dirt and dust that beset most Indian cities.

Besides its unusual geography, the town gets its character from the layer upon layer of cultural influence. For over 500 years, foreigners have been pitching up in this part of Kerala, which could be considered the West's gateway to the whole country. Fort Kochi was where colonial Europe first stuck its flag into Indian soil, and the place gets a mention in Chinese books predating even that. The Portuguese, who ruled during the 16th century and half of the 17th century, were followed by the Dutch, then the Mysore (a kingdom in Southern India), and finally by the British Raj. All left their indelible stamp on the place. Throw in Jew Town and some Chinese fishing nets (of which more later), and it starts to become clear why Kochi is such a compelling architectural and cultural hybrid. The various nationalities that have trundled their way through town are responsible not only for many of Kochi's attractions, but also its sophisticated gastronomic scene; the town can definitely stake a convincing claim to offer the best food in the state.

At the centre of the action is Ernakulam, part of the mainland. The rest of the conurbation is made up of a confluence of small islands and peninsulas divided by Vembanad Lake. Of greatest interest to the visitor

⬖ *The pleasant streets of Fort Kochi make for an enjoyable stroll*

will be the stretch of land that hosts Fort Kochi, Mattancherry and Jew Town, steeped in history and atmosphere and home to some of the main attractions. Willingdon Island (also known as Wellington Island), which sits between Ernakulam and Fort Kochi, contains some of the metropolis's more exclusive accommodation.

BEACHES

Most tourists come to Kochi for its urban attractions, rather than the beach. As a working port, tankers ply the waterways continuously, so this is not the place for a serene dip in pristine seas. However, the rocky and rough-hewn **Fort Kochi Beach** can be found 2 km ($1^1/_4$ miles) from the boat jetty at Ernakulam. Surrounding the beach are the usual complement of coconut trees and a few places to get a bite to eat. Athletic Kochiites often indulge in a spot of beach cricket and volleyball. If you're exceptionally lucky with your timing you might spot a dolphin. A more certain sight is the Chinese fishing nets that pepper the coastline (see page 45). Another pleasant beach can be found over on Vypin Island (see page 79).

THINGS TO SEE & DO

Art galleries

As Kerala's most cosmopolitan city, art lovers will find plenty of places to browse and buy. Here are a few of the best in the area:

Dravidian Art and Performance Gallery showcases local art and hosts concerts in high season at 18.00. ⓐ Bazaar Road, south of customs jetty, Fort Kochi ⓣ (0484) 309 6812 ⓛ 09.00–17.00

Kerala Lalit Kala Akademy (Kerala Academy of Art) hosts temporary exhibitions of modern art, copies of antediluvian works and royal paraphernalia. ⓐ Darbar Hall, Darbar Hall Road, off MG Road, Ernakulam ⓛ Usually 10.00–20.00 daily

Kashi Art Gallery displays local work and is also home to a pleasant café. ⓐ Burgher Street, Fort Kochi ⓣ (0484) 221 5769 ⓦ kashiartgallery.com ⓔ mail@kashiartgallery.com ⓛ 10.00–12.30 & 14.00–18.00 daily

⬢ *Standing guard at the entrance to the Dutch Palace*

Chinese fishing nets

These extraordinary looking contraptions are probably the most distinctive symbol of Kochi. Large, shore-operated lift nets, they work through a complicated system of counterweights and ropes. Despite their considerable size (they are typically more than 10 m (33 ft) tall and the nets 20 m (66 ft) wide), the cantilever system nets only a few fish, but with the whole process taking just a few minutes, there can be repeated catches throughout the day, depending on the tide. It is thought that it was 14th-century Chinese explorer Zheng He who introduced the nets to the city – hence the name – and Kochi's role as a hub of the spice industry lends some credence to the possibility. Picturesque at any time, the nets are particularly pretty at sunset, but the most interesting sight to see is the teamwork and mechanics when they are in use.

ⓐ Fort Kochi and at other points around Vembanad Lake

Dutch Palace

Somewhat confusingly, given the name, this medieval site was built by the Portuguese in the Keralan style, and presented to the Raja of Kochi in 1555. The Dutch renovated it over a century later, hence its moniker. You might also hear it referred to as Mattancherry Palace. Its chief draw is its fabulous murals, dazzling depictions of Hindu gods, whose detail is quite astounding. Other rooms play host to portraits of the city's rajas (in a somewhat incongruous European style), an impressive-looking palanquin and various other royal paraphernalia. It's all accompanied by informative English captions. Official guides are on hand if you're interested in further explanation.

ⓐ Junction of Bazaar Road and Palace Road, Kochi 🕐 (0484) 222 6085 🕓 10.00–17.00 Sat–Thur, closed Fri ❶ Admission charge; photography not allowed

Hill Palace Museum

The Kochi royals' old pad now holds their memorabilia, some 19th-century art and other regal knick-knacks.

Clamorous and captivating, a kathakali *performance is a Keralan delight*

ⓐ Tripunithura, 12 km (7½ miles) southeast of Ernakulam
ⓘ (0484) 278 1113 ⓛ 09.00–16.30 Tues–Sun, closed Mon; may close for lunch from 12.30–14.00 ⓝ A bus goes there from Ernakulam's MG Road

Indo-Portuguese Museum

Portugal's influence on the region, particularly in terms of religion, is showcased in this historical site, which has been functioning as a museum for over a century.

ⓐ Bishop's House, Fort Kochi ⓘ (0484) 221 5400 ⓛ 09.00–13.00 & 14.00–18.00 Tues–Sun, closed Mon ⓘ Admission charge

Jew Town

Jews are believed to have been trading in Kerala as far back as biblical times. Though few of them remain, this historical part of Kochi has retained its distinctive atmosphere and is a thriving tourist area. Originally it was a centre of the city's spice trade, and the residue of that industry is detectable in the air. However, most of the cumin and ginger has now given way to tourist shops full of saris, fabrics and the usual Indian wares, from where traders give the hard sell to passing foreigners. This can begin to grate after the fifteenth 'no, thank you', but the area has enough charm to compensate, and there are plenty of cafés and restaurants on whose upstairs balconies you can take respite from the retail hustle and admire the view. The focal point of the area is the **Pardesi Synagogue**, the oldest in the Commonwealth. This peaceful place of worship is well worth dropping into to see the Belgian glass chandeliers. But don't forget to look down; the floor is covered with hand-painted Chinese tiles, each of which is unique. As in all synagogues, Scrolls of the Law and Golden Crowns are kept on site. Pardesi Synagogue ⓐ Jew Town Road ⓛ 10.00–12.00 & 15.00–17.00 Sun–Thur, closed Fri & Sat ⓘ Admission charge; closed Jewish holidays

Kathakali

Kochi is the centre of Kerala's spectacular dance-dramas – the *kathakali*. Authenticity may have been sacrificed at the altar of tourist appetites (in its traditional form performances could go on for several hours – for visitors it has been condensed to just under an hour), but it would still be a travesty to come to Kerala without experiencing this spectacular form of entertainment. The actors (men also play female roles) spend a couple of hours readying themselves before going onstage. The make-up is an art form in itself, and some performances include viewing the application of cosmetics as part of the fun. Proceedings then begin in earnest with a demonstration of some of the eye, head and body movements involved, followed by the nine different emotions depicted. The main course is the acting out of a dramatic and usually violent fable, culminating in much screaming and dashing from side to side. It's a flabbergasting spectacle – although be warned that very young children are liable to be scared out of their wits by the end!

Kerala *Kathakali* Centre ⓐ Opposite Brunton Boatyard, KB Jacob Road, Fort Kochi ⓣ (0484) 221 5827 ⓦ www.kathakalicentre.com ⓔ vijayan@kathakalicentre.com ⓛ 18.00 daily ❶ Admission charge

Kochi Cultural Centre ⓐ Sangamam, Manikath Road, Fort Kochi ⓣ (0484) 235 6366 ⓦ www.kochiculturalcentre.com ⓔ director@kochiculturalcentre.com ⓛ 18.30 daily ❶ Admission charge

Kodanad elephant training camp
Elephant rides and other pachyderm-related fun. Get there at 08.00 to assist with bath time.
ⓐ 50 km (31 miles) from Kochi, off Vallom Panamkuzhi Road ⓛ 07.00–18.00 daily ❶ No admission charge except for rides; guides appreciate a tip

Santa Cruz Basilica
Atmospheric chanting, ornate statues and murals – including a large Last Supper scene at the front – lend this church its impressive atmosphere. Don't forget to look up for the crucifixion scenes on the ceiling. Originally built by the Portuguese in 1505, the current building is over a hundred years old. An English-speaking custodian is sometimes

on hand to fill visitors in on the history. The attached school, with its gaggle of excited children to-ing and fro-ing, is another attraction.
ⓐ KB Jacob Road, Fort Kochi ⓣ (0484) 222 5799 ⓛ 09.00–13.00 & 15.00–17.00 daily

St Francis Church

India's oldest European church, built in 1503 by the Portuguese, is a bright, attractive venue, with simple chandeliers and stained-glass windows. Famed Portuguese explorer Vasco da Gama, who died on a visit to Kochi, was buried here before his remains were repatriated.
ⓐ Bastion Street, Fort Kochi ⓛ 09.30–13.00, 14.30–17.00 Mon–Fri; 14.30–17.00 Sat, closed Sun

◔ *The pretty Santa Cruz Basilica is more than a hundred years old*

TAKING A BREAK

The Armoury ££ ❶ Enviable harbour views make this café-bar a lovely spot for afternoon chai (choose from an impressive selection of teas) and home-made cake, or have a beer and watch the world go by. ⓐ Brunton Boatyard, Fort Kochi ⓣ (0484) 221 5461 ⓛ 07.30–22.30 daily

Café Crafters ££ ❷ The upstairs café at this antiques shop serves up sandwiches and soups as well as more traditionally Indian fare. There's also a range of refreshing drinks including milkshakes and some rather tempting cakes. Choose one of the three tables on the balcony – if they're free – and watch Jew Town go by while you eat. ⓐ 6/141 Jew Town Road ⓣ (0484) 222 3346 ⓦ www.crafters.in ⓔ crafters@vsnl.net ⓛ 08.00–18.30 daily

Cocoa Tree ££ ❸ Coffees, pastries, breads, snacks and light lunches are served until late in this stylish hotel café. ⓐ 39/2026 The Avenue Regent, MG Road, Ernakulam ⓣ (0484) 237 7977 ⓛ Until 01.00 daily

Coffee Beanz ££ ❹ Part of a popular chain with a handful of outlets throughout the state – as the deliberate misspelling suggests, this place is brimming with youthful attitude. ⓐ Shanmugam Road, Ernakulam ⓣ (0484) 235 1677 ⓛ 11.30–22.30 daily

Kashi Art Café ££ ❺ Enjoy coffee, cakes and other tempting light bites with the arty set in Kashi's lushly pleasant garden. A daily changing menu keeps things fresh. ⓐ Burgher Street, Fort Kochi ⓣ (0484) 221 5769 ⓦ www.kashiartgallery.com ⓔ mail@kashiartgallery.com ⓛ 08.30–19.30 daily

AFTER DARK

Chariot Beach ££ ❻ It can take a while to get served, but the large number of tourists that make this the case are testament to its

Take a break at the Brunton Boatyard Hotel

popularity. Watch your seafood being cooked on the outdoor grill, or play it safe with foreign favourites like Italian, Chinese or classic Indian dishes. ⓐ Corner of Princess Street, near Children's Park, Fort Kochi ⓣ (0484) 221 7807, 984 705 7745 ⓛ 08.00–23.00 daily ⓘ No alcohol

Four Seasons ££ ❼   A little piece of Europe in India, this upstairs Mediterranean hotel-restaurant apes Italian style in a big way, right down to the red-and-white check table clothes. Take a break from curry and choose from a range of reasonably priced pizza, pasta and salads. The restaurant does not currently serve alcohol but may get a licence this year. ⓐ 1/644 Princess Street, behind the post office, Fort Kochi ⓣ (0484) 311 5672 ⓦ www.fourseasonskochi.com ⓔ info@fourseasonskochi.com ⓛ 08.30–10.30, 12.00–15.00 & 18.00–23.00 daily

History restaurant £££ ❶   Drawing on the cuisines of the various traders who have wended their way through Kochi over the centuries, this heritage hotel restaurant offers a melange of Dutch, Syrian Christian, British, Indian and Keralan fare, using historical recipes. Meanwhile, the morning's catch is served in its stylish Terrace Grill. ⓐ Brunton Boatyard, Fort Kochi ⓣ (0484) 221 5461 ⓛ 19.30–22.30 or 23.00 daily

Loungevity £££ ❸   Clubbing opportunities are practically non-existent in Kerala (Goa takes care of the nightlife for the bottom half of India), so anyone yearning for a spot of late-night action can get their fix in the state's first-ever designer bar. Plenty of trendy glass and form-over-function type furniture seal its cool credentials. Music varies from chill-out to Michael Jackson. ⓐ 39/2026 The Avenue Regent, MG Road, Ernakulam ⓣ (0484) 237 7977 ⓛ 19.00–late daily

Calicut

It was near Kerala's third-largest urban area, once known as the 'city of spices', that Portuguese explorer Vasco da Gama first set foot in India. Calicut was in past times the most important port on the Malabar Coast. It no longer plays the strategic role it did, but the former capital still has its industry, notably spices and coconuts, and consequently the bustling atmosphere of trade and commerce.

Calicut (the anglicised version of Kozhikode) is not a compelling stop on the tourist trail, but makes a pleasant place to pass through. Its charms have been recognised by a research company, which ranked it the second-best Indian city in which to live. There's a sizeable Muslim contingent here, and some of the main points of interests are the local mosques. Calicut also has a sprinkling of cultural attractions and some quintessentially Indian water tanks. But the main pleasure is simply walking around the narrow, curious alleyways and taking in the atmosphere.

BEACHES

Calicut's beach is refreshingly untouched by the driving force of commercialisation. It's an unusually large expanse of sand, big enough to contain a football pitch and separated from the main road, which also doubles as a wide promenade, by a sporadic line of trees. There is plenty of space to find a solitary spot, although the rare appearance of foreign visitors may result in some friendly approaches from local beachgoers. As throughout much of the north of Kerala, it might not be the most sensitive move to whip off your clothes for a spot of sunbathing. Instead, this beach's pleasures lie in watching the fishing boats go about their daily work, maybe catching some beach football and admiring the view. There is little in the way of landmarks – no sculptures here – aside from two rickety piers, which date back over a century, and a lighthouse. If the kids are in tow, there's a small playground called **Lions Park** and an additional entertainment is **Marine Water Aquarium**. If you're there before 18.00 you can catch a nice sunset.

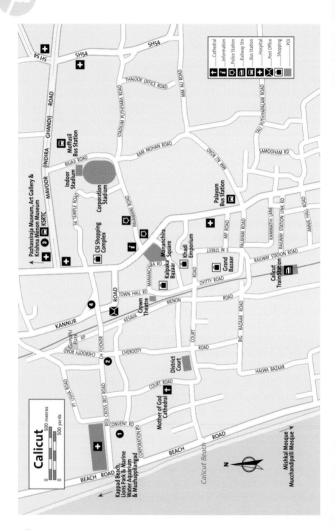

History buffs prepared to make the 16-km (10-mile) trip northwards will enjoy a visit to **Kappad Beach** (sometimes called Kappakkadavu). In 1498, Vasco da Gama and 170 of his men landed their three boats on this beach, heralding the start of the European intervention that would leave a profound mark on both state and country. The Zamorin (the local ruler) did not take kindly to the Portuguese arrival, and slung da Gama in jail. Eventually negotiations over trade terms began, but often descended into violence and the Europeans later based themselves elsewhere. Today the momentous events are marked by nothing more than a small stone monument. An 800-year-old temple on the rocks close by is another draw.

THINGS TO SEE & DO

Mananchira Square

This square that is Calicut's centrepiece takes its name from the large spring-fed lake in its middle, which in turn is named after one of the Zamorins, the powerful rulers who ran Kerala from the 14th to the 18th century. The quintessentially Indian artificial lake once served a palace. Popular with local bathers, it is a striking presence in Calicut and one of the town's most aesthetically pleasing features. The square's main gate is also impressively grand. Around the square are an open-air theatre, musical fountain, quirky statues, and several important civic buildings. The meandering backstreets, with their air of old India, are fun to explore. Although generally used by local families as an evening hangout, the square is occasionally given over to events. It is scheduled to be renovated in 2010 and may be closed to the public for a while.

Mosques

Calicut's Muslim population erected some of its main landmarks. The 650-year-old **Mishkal** or **Misqalpalli Mosque** has a hint of the Far East about it, thanks mainly to its stepped roof. It takes its name from the rich Arab trader at whose behest it was built. The building, one of Kerala's

Taking an afternoon promenade in the sun on the beach at Calicut

oldest mosques, still bears traces of an attack by the Portuguese in 1510, which left it ablaze. The five-storey structure can accommodate several hundred worshippers at a time.

Mishkal Mosque ❸ Kuttichira, north of the water tank

The nearby **Mucchandipalli Mosque** is of a similar style. Tourists don't normally enter, but you can have a wander round outside and can often catch a glimpse of the devotees. The maze of narrow streets in the neighbourhood is interesting to explore.

Mucchandipalli Mosque ❸ Kuttichira, north of the water tank

Museums

Conveniently located together in a small complex, enabling you to do all the cultural stuff in one fell swoop, are two museums and a gallery.

The **Pazhassiraja Museum** takes its name from Pazhassi Raja, a local hero who led an uprising against the British and came to be known as the Lion of Kerala. On display are a gamut of small-scale models of temples, coins, tools, pots, palanquins, hats and other artefacts. The best stuff is in the basement, which houses an impressive array of statues.

❸ East Hill, 5 km (3 miles) from town ⏰ 10.00–17.00 Tues–Sun, closed Mon ❶ Admission charge

A short walk away are the **Art Gallery** and **Krishna Menon Museum**, where art lovers can peruse local works, including oils by 19th-century Keralan painter Raja Ravi Varma, whose creations are an interesting blend of Indian traditions and the European school. Vengalil Krishnan Krishna Menon, from whom the museum takes its name, was a nationalist politician who spent much of his life in the UK before being appointed to lead the Indian delegation to the United Nations, where he was a thorn in the side of the USA. He still holds the record for the longest speech ever given in the United Nations Security Council – an unprecedented 8 hours! The museum charts his life and work.

⏰ 10.00–17.00 Tues & Thur–Sun, 13.00–17.00 Wed, closed Mon ❶ Admission charge

TAKING A BREAK

French Bakery £ ❶ Don't let the rather misleading name – it's not French and it's a restaurant rather than a bakery – put you off: this popular, upstairs joint provides filling and well-received snacks and meals to a happy crowd. ⓐ Between Corporation Road and Convent Road ❶ (0495) 236 5366 ❶ 09.30–18.30 Mon–Sat, closed Sun

Coffee Beanz ££ ❷ Since the popular chain opened in Calicut in 2007, this place has been serving up great coffee, snacks and meals to a loyal following. ⓐ 11/506A Venmarath Building, corner of Cherooty Road and Red Cross (RC) Road ❶ (0495) 409 9799 ❶ 12.00–24.00 Tues, Wed, Fri–Sun, 12.00–00.15 Mon, 12.30–24.00 Thur

AFTER DARK

Sagar £ ❸ Be prepared to wait at this bustling, bargain, family-orientated eatery. Ginger or garlic chicken and pathri, appam, fish curries and the various vegetarian masalas are the highlights on the menu, which also includes Chinese and European dishes. There's another branch on the same road. ⓐ Mavoor (also known as Indira Gandhi, or IG) Road, near the KSRTC bus stand ❶ (0495) 272 0152 ❶ 06.00–02.00 daily

Paragon ££ ❹ Operating since 1939, Paragon is ever-popular on the variable Calicut restaurant scene. The extensive menu features a wealth of Malabari, North Indian, Chinese and continental dishes, including mouth-watering mussels, which can be hard to find in Kerala due to the locals not being that keen on them. Station yourself in the air-conditioned room and try the famous fish *kombathu* and rice cakes. ⓐ Kannur Road, corner with RC Road ❶ (0495) 276 7020 ⓦ www.paragonrestaurant.net ⓔ mail@paragonrestaurant.net

Calicut's Islamic heritage is in evidence at the 650-year-old Mishkal Mosque

Muzhappilangad

Neglected by the guidebooks, Muzhappilangad is the place to go if you really want to get off the beaten track and enjoy the pleasures of the Keralan coast in their unadulterated form. Commercialism is utterly unknown here, and it can be difficult even to find a restaurant or hotel. What business there is comes in the form of fishing and picking coconuts – this is the kind of area that has one designated coconut picker per village. In Muzhappilangad you can see scenes of Indian life that have changed little over the past decades, if not centuries. With the first European tourists starting to come just a decade ago, foreigners here are so scarce that your appearance will enthuse the local children and you are likely to attract a small following when passing by the villager's homes. At a slight remove from the beach, people live in small houses in the dense wood, and walking around in this area can be almost as much of a pleasure as the beach itself.

BEACHES

Muzhappilangad is home to the oddity that is Kerala's first drive-in beach (said to be the longest drive-in beach in Asia, no less), something that is wildly popular with local people but can seem odd to tourists. Of the 5-km (3-mile) stretch of sand, cars are permitted to zoom along a 4-km (2½-mile) strip. Once you shake off the feeling that you're committing an environmental transgression and doing something, well, naughty, it's actually a fun and liberating feeling to drive up and down by the sea. You may want to avoid peak visiting times, though, for fear of getting embroiled in a seaside traffic jam.

Ignoring the vehicles plying it, verdant Muzhappilangad Beach is one of Kerala's finest. Approached through a winding road amidst coconut groves, the beach is naturally bordered by black rocks. This has the effect of shielding it from currents, and the water can be gentle, should you wish to swim – but bear in mind that there won't be a lifeguard. Where the beach meets the road, the Muzhappilangad Tourism Information

Centre claims to offer particulars about the area, but may be more useful for the toilets. There are no artistic sculptures on the beach, but a large hammer-and-sickle monument means you can't forget the area's Communist proclivities.

Away from the main drag, there are smaller coves where you can enjoy absolute privacy in a tropical idyll. At low tide, it is possible to walk to Dharmadam Island, a 2-hectare (5-acre) islet and former Buddhist stronghold, which can be seen from the beach. But be sure to check the tide times to avoid getting cut off from the mainland, as the sea level rises rapidly.

THINGS TO SEE & DO

The beauty of Muzhappilangad is that there is nothing to do, aside from enjoy your surroundings! What eateries there are, are of the local 'meals' kind, and if you're staying in the area your guesthouse will probably take care of feeding you. For beachside refreshments, there are a few stalls set up where the approach road meets the sand, close to the tourist centre.

🔺 *The lesser-trod reaches of northern Kerala boast perfect, palm-fringed beaches*

Kannur

By the time you reach northern Kerala, tourists begin to thin out, and Kannur is probably the last hub for visitors before you begin to go seriously off the beaten track. Previously known by the European name Cannanore, you'll often still hear it referred to as such. Historically, the town was strategically important. In the middle ages it was the capital of the Kolathiri Rajas and prior to that was a key Arabian Sea port, trading with Persia and Arabia. Kannur's industrial credentials even earned praise from no less figure than fêted explorer Marco Polo, who dubbed the port a 'great emporium of spice trade'. Its kudos may have waned since its prestigious past, but it still retains significance. Kerala's fourth-largest city is home to some noteworthy military sites – past and present – the most striking of which is the Portuguese-built St Angelo's Fort.

Islam has also had a hand in shaping the town's architecture and atmosphere. The seat of the Arakkal royal family, the only Muslim dynasty in the state, is now a visitor attraction. In fact, from Kannur northwards things get much more Islamic. But Hindu traditions still thrive: northern Kerala is the home of *theyyam*, a colourful ritual that rivals even *kathakali* for its vibrancy. Other cultural influences come from familiar sources: the Portuguese, Dutch and British all tinkered with the place at one time or another.

The self-proclaimed 'land of looms and lore' (the area is a heartland of the handloom industry) has another accomplishment: taking into account various standard-of-living categories, a research company proclaimed it one of the top ten places to live in India. Cashews and weaving are also big business here. As a relatively large city, different areas have their distinctive characters – some parts are military, others industrial, others pleasantly open and green.

BEACHES

Kannur's pleasing beaches cater more to local visitors than foreign tourists, and you may find yourself the object of local curiosity, though it

◔ Cooling off with an ice cream on the beach at Kannur

will always be good-natured. As is the case pretty much throughout the less touristy north of the state, unless you are particularly unabashed, the beaches here are probably best enjoyed in modest attire. Unusually, the town's main beaches have been turned into pay areas, with set 'opening hours'. In practice, this is unlikely to affect you (unless you wanted to take a moonlit walk): the timings are pretty much daylight hours and the entrance charge is always nominal.

Baby Beach

The child-phobic need not fear; Baby Beach gets its name because it is smaller than its adjacent stretch of shoreline, Payyambalam, not because it is teeming with toddlers. This is another pretty, tree-lined cove, backed by dense greenery, which tails off into rocks. Part of the Cannanore Cantonment, it is occasionally off limits to the public.

ⓐ Adjacent to St Angelo's Fort, 3 km (2 miles) northeast of Kannur

Lighthouse Beach & Sea View Park

Its name is something of a misnomer, as you won't find a beach as such. Rather, this is a shoreline promenade, with a touch of the English Riviera about it. The lengthy walkway meanders, creating natural secluded coves beloved of courting couples enjoying a romantic sunset. Dotted along it are benches, from where you can sit and enjoy the charming view out over the sea and rocks below. More intrepid sorts can even climb down the rocks themselves, and get closer to the waterline, though there isn't a proper walkway. The red-and-white Cannanore Lighthouse can also be visited for a couple of hours in the afternoon.

ⓐ 1 km (²/₃ mile) from Kannur town 🕒 09.00–20.00 daily
❶ Admission charge
Cannanore Lighthouse 🕒 15.00–17.00 daily or one hour before sunset, whichever is earlier ❶ Admission charge

Payyambalam Beach Garden

Understandably popular with locals is Kannur's beach garden. The entrance leads onto a pleasant grassy knoll that boasts a children's play

area and several statues, including beach sculpture favourite Kanayi Kunhiraman's *Mother and Child*. The garden is a great spot to revive yourself, with plenty of places for a sit down (the most popular of which are in the shade of some welcome trees) and a refreshments kiosk. A nod to Kannur's military links is found in the form of a model tank – rather incongruous given the laid-back, leisurely vibe. Cross the grass and you'll come to a river, which divides the green area from the beach itself. Over the bridge is a collection of memorial monuments and statues, in keeping with the serenity of the area. A little further on lies the splendid beach, a long, wide and clean stretch of sand that often plays host to impromptu cricket matches. There's a picnic table, various stalls selling drinks, fruit and cashews, and ice cream vendors cycle up and down
ⓐ 2 km (1¼ miles) from Kannur town ⓛ 08.00–20.00 daily
ⓘ Admission charge

🔺 *Sculpture embellishes Payyambalam Beach Garden*

Thottada Beach

Attached to Costa Malabari resort, Thottada is another typically beautiful beach.

🄰 7 km (4 miles) southeast of Kannur

THINGS TO SEE & DO

Arakkal Museum

Kerala's only Muslim ruling family are commemorated in this, their former palatial home. The Arakkal Ali Rajas' furniture, weapons, books and sundry regal odds and ends are on display, along with early telephones and telescopes. A panel in English fills visitors in on the family's interesting back story.

🄰 Ayikkara, 2 km (1¼ miles) from Kannur town 🕒 08.00–18.00 Tues–Sat, closed Mon ❶ Admission charge

St Angelo's Fort

Constructed by the Portuguese in 1505, and later passing through the ownership of the Dutch, the Arakkal Royal Family and the British, Kannur's landmark attraction is worth visiting as much for its fabulous views as for the building itself. Approached through a peaceful wooded area with stunning banyan trees, the fort itself today has a tranquil feel, far removed from its military roots. This is due in part to the Indian visitors, who use the place as a garden as much as a cultural site; it's particularly popular for wedding photos.

Parts of the fort are relatively well preserved, and you can see the remainder of a chapel, hospital, jail and barracks, an interesting Flemish epitaph, as well as a surfeit of cannons. An unexpected delight is the abundance of wildlife. Fifty species of butterfly are said to frequent the area, as well as cuckoos, eagles, hawks, hummingbirds, owls, cranes and kingfishers. Foreign visitors are sometimes escorted round by a friendly guide.

🄰 3 km (2 miles) from Kannur town 🕒 08.00–18.00 daily ❶ Admission is free but there is a charge to park

Theyyam

Boasting 7,000 years of history, and believed to have originated before Hinduism, *theyyam* was born out of early harvest festival customs. It involves an elaborately attired male dancer – replete with extravagant make-up, jewellery, headdress and multi-coloured costume – being 'possessed' by a female god, to manic dancing and drumming. Proceedings, which are usually held at a village shrine, can continue for 12, even 24 hours – although mercifully the performers are allowed breaks. *Theyyam* is a seasonally practised ritual which takes place from October to May. It has not had the same tourist-fuelled industry spring up around it as *kathakali*, so it can be harder to track down a performance, especially with the village locations. Enquire locally if

🔺 *St Angelo's Fort offers history with a stunning panorama*

you're interested in seeing some: the Malayalam newspapers may contain details, or ask at your hotel. If you're prepared to undertake a bit of a trek, the **Kerala Folklore Academi** stages performances, along with other ritual state art forms – Kolam Thullal, Garudan Hanging and Chavittu Nadakam.

Kerala Folklore Academi ⓐ Near Chirakkal Pond, Valapattanam ⓣ (0497) 277 8090 ⓔ nambiar_ak@yahoo.com

Workers' cooperatives

While the northern reaches of the state have far fewer tourist amenities, the upside of that is that they afford a glimpse of Keralan life as it is lived by the Keralans. An important aspect of that is industry, in particular the workers' collectives that reflect the state's Communist leanings. The long-established Loknath Weavers' Industrial Co-op Society – a manufacturer of the handloom products for which the area is famous – offers tours in English and has an on-site shop selling its products. Smokers (who don't generally have the best time in this anti-tobacco state) may like to check out Kerala Dinesh Beedi Workers' Central Co-op Society. Taking its name from the *beedi*, the thin leaf cigarette, the group has now expanded into areas as diverse as IT, curry powder and umbrellas. Its factory is in Thottada.

Loknath Weavers' Industrial Co-op Society ⓐ 2.5 km (1½ miles) from Kannur town on the Kannur-Thalassery road ⓣ (0497) 272 6330 ⓦ www.lokfab.com ⓔ lokweave@yahoo.com ⓛ 09.00–17.30 Mon–Sat, closed Sun

Kerala Dinesh Beedi Workers' Central Co-op Society ⓐ Thottada, 7 km (4½ miles) south of Kannur ⓣ (0497) 270 1699 ⓦ www.keraladinesh.com ⓔ dineshltd@gmail.com ⓛ 08.00–17.00 Tues–Sat, closed Sun & Mon

TAKING A BREAK

Kannur is not overburdened with eateries catering to the tourist contingent, and many hotels and guesthouses make up for this by feeding visitors themselves, with meals included in the room rates.

Bharath Restaurant £ Vegetarian fare is the thing at this intimate and low-priced hotel eatery. The cuisine is old-school Keralan, with the local bread getting special plaudits. ⓐ CW-1228 Station Road, near Central Bank of India ⓣ (0497) 276 8191 ⓛ 11.30–15.30, 16.00–21.30 Mon–Sat, closed Sun

Indian Coffee House £ Local outlet of the famous cooperative chain serving its standard range of coffees (as you'd expect), teas, juices, breakfasts, snacks and Indian staples. At these prices, you just cannot go wrong. ⓐ Near KSRTC Bus Stand ⓣ 944 754 0294 ⓛ 06.00–22.00

Lighthouse Beach Ice Cream Parlour £ At the top of the headland, a raised garden is home to this small ice cream parlour, with a handful of tables and chairs outside. ⓐ Sea View Park ⓛ 09.00–20.00 (approx)

Mareena Bakery £ Traditional Keralan and north Malabar desserts are served along with a selection of rolls and pastries. ⓐ Poothappara, Kannur-Azhikkal Road, about 5 km (3 miles) from Kannur town ⓣ 974 488 0707

Payyambalam Beach Garden Kiosk £ This small kiosk sells drinks, crisps, sweets and ice cream. There are no tables, but the garden has plenty of seats where you can sit a while and consume your refreshments. ⓐ At the entrance to Payyambalam Beach Garden, opposite the ticket booth ⓛ 08.00–20.00 (approx)

Kasaragod

Kerala's northernmost reaches are close to uncharted territory on the tourist map – a situation that is unlikely to continue indefinitely as they are home to some picture-perfect beaches. Kasaragod town – and the district that shares the same name – have a markedly different feel from the lower end of the state, and southerners even have some difficulty in understanding Malayalam as it is spoken here. In fact, the Keralan tongue is one of seven languages spoken by substantial numbers here. Much of the different feel is down to the area's Muslim population. Mosques are chief among the local landmarks; some temples too are worth seeing. The town itself is not the most attractive, but it's a good jumping-off point for some superb coastline and the famous Bekal Fort. The twelve rivers that criss-cross the district also lend the wider area plenty of aesthetic appeal.

BEACHES

Kasaragod's Muslim fishermen enjoy high local renown, and a visit to the fine-looking beach is repaid by seeing them in action. The shoreline runs, largely uninterrupted, from Kasaragod town all the way to Bekal, about 10 km (6 miles) down the coast, whose fort is the main point of interest in the area. Though the beach has a pristine appearance, the cleanliness of the local water, as well as local sensibilities, make swimming unwise.

The coastline in this area is often referred to locally as Kadappara Beach (the Malayalam word for seashore). Of this stretch, the so-called CPCRI beach (named after the Central Plantation Crops Research Institute

PACK A PICNIC
Outside a few standard eateries in the town centre, restaurants are scarce in these parts, so if you're heading out for a day at the beach, it's a good idea to pack provisions.

▲ A Kasaragod mosque nestled among the trees

nearby), 4 km (2¹/₂ miles) from the main town, is particularly appealing. Other sections worthy of note are Bekal Beach, accessed via a pleasant park, for which there is a small entry charge. Very popular locally, it can get crowded with families at weekends. Kappil Beach, 6 km (3³/₄ miles) to the north of Bekal, is another stunner, but take care, as the sandbars move with the tide and you can easily find yourself out of your depth.

THINGS TO SEE & DO

Bekal Fort

Kerala's biggest fort spans 16 hectares (40 acres) on a high promontory. It was built quickly in the 17th century by the Nayaka clan of Karnataka (the state to the north) for defensive purposes, and the strategic features, such as tactically sited holes for firing on an approaching enemy, are among the points of interest, along with the tunnel, tank, tower and ammunition magazine. After passing through various Indian hands the fort ended up under the ownership of the British East India Company, and a British rest house has survived at the site. Bekal Fort enjoys some splendid sea views, particularly from atop the observation tower.
ⓐ 12 km (7¹/₂ miles) north of Kanhangad ⓣ 08.00–17.00 daily
ⓦ www.bekal.com ⓘ Admission charge

Mosques and temples

Its Islamic places of worship are among Kasaragod's few landmarks. Nellikunnu Mosque, close to the town, Theruvatthu Mosque on MG Road and Malik Deenar Mosque in the Thalankara area are the main ones, and attract numerous devotees during Uroos festivals. Madhur Temple, which sits beside the Madhuvahini river, 6.5 km (4 miles) from Kasaragod, is another striking religious building, thanks to its turrets, gables and imposing copper-plate roof.

◗ *Kerala's stunning backwaters have a dreamy other-worldly quality*

EXCURSIONS
Out & about

Periyar National Park

High up in the Cardamom Hills of the Western Ghats, Periyar is one of the shining stars of Keralan tourism. The park was developed around an artificial lake engineered by the British at the end of the 19th century. The entire protected area spreads out over 777 sq km (300 sq miles), just under half of which has been designated national park, with a sizeable area open to the public. Although it's sometimes referred to as Periyar Tiger Reserve (along with other monikers such as Thekkady and Kumili), you'd have to be incredibly fortunate to spot a stripy big cat prowling around, as they number in the low double figures. Elephant sightings are much more likely, however, and Indian bison, sambar and wild boar may also show their faces. Birds, reptiles, fish, insects and amphibians are in plentiful supply.

ⓐ 4 km (2½ miles) from Kumili in Idukki district ☎ (04869) 224 571
ⓦ www.periyartigerreserve.org ⓔ mail@periyartigerreserve.org
🕓 07.00–18.00 daily

THINGS TO SEE & DO

Wildlife spotting

Various boat trips are offered in the area – an expedient way of spotting wildlife as all animals have to drink. Visitors can also trek, from brief sallies to hardcore days-long hikes complete with camping. The less adventurous or energetically inclined can see Periyar in a four-wheel drive, and stay in one of the many lodges.

Useful information centres include: **DTPC office** (☎ (04869) 222 620 🕓 10.00–17.00 Mon–Sat, closed Sun), **Ecotourism centre** (☎ (04869) 224 571 🕓 09.00–17.00 daily) and **Forest Department** (☎ (04869) 222 028 🕓 06.00–18.00 daily).

Abraham's Spice Garden

Once you've had your fill of the Periyar area's wildlife, turn your attention to its plant life. There are few things more quintessentially Indian than

spices, and Kumily, close to the sanctuary, offers the opportunity to immerse yourself in spice world. Tours of Abraham's Spice Garden, which has been operating for 60 years, include insights into crops from cocoa to cardamom, and also take in the Ayurveda garden.
3 km (just under 2 miles) due south of Kumily (04869) 222919
www.abrahamspice.com info@abrahamspice.com 06.30–19.00
Admission charge

TAKING A BREAK

If you're on a long trek, food is normally provided by the tour company; otherwise, there are some places to eat close to the park entrance.

You're likely to see elephants in Periyar National Park

Backwaters

If you take one excursion away from the beach resorts during your Kerala sojourn, make it a backwater cruise. The system of palm-fringed rivers, canals, lakes and lagoons is a mystical delight, an entire other kingdom on the water. The science part is interesting – created by wave movements and currents, the backwaters now have a unique, brackish ecosystem. But the real fun is to be had in just plodding along in the boat, exchanging friendly waves with residents and other water-bound tourists and enjoying the peek into village and river life the backwaters afford. Your accommodation is likely to take the form of a *kettuvallam*, a picturesque houseboat with a thatched roof. Many (400 are said to sail the waters) are quite luxurious. At the other end of the pecuniary scale, it's also possible to do a similar jaunt by ferry. Various routes are possible: you can embark and return to the same point, while some tourists use the backwaters as a leg on their journey and continue from a different dropping-off point. Most houseboats will incorporate land-based excursions into their itinerary. These fascinating outings can include visits to villages, places of worship, schools, homes and markets. The main action is in the south of the state, in Kuttanad, but the off-the-beaten-track brigade may be interested to hear of the Valiaparamba Backwaters, further north, between Kannur and Kasaragod. A few of the major towns on the southern backwaters are listed below.

THINGS TO SEE & DO

Alappuzha

Bordering Vembanad (India's longest lake), Alappuzha has attracted comparisons with Venice (although they are perhaps a little flattering). The port's waterways are relentlessly busy, and it's a major gateway to the backwaters. If you find yourself passing through, there are a couple of temples of note and a pleasant beach. The several boat races that are held here would also be worth a diversion.

◔ *A backwaters excursion reveals Keralan life on the water*

Kollam

The ancient Malabar Coastal port of Kollam may no longer have the commercial standing it once did, but it remains a lively market town, given a mellow side by the surrounding cashew and coconut plantations. Meandering streets are home to historical wooden houses that hint at the town's colonial past. The large beach, 2 km (1¼ miles) south of town, is enlivened by a bustling fish market and the bazaar in town sells oddities from sacks of chillies to severed goats' heads.

Kottayam

Earning the moniker of the 'City of Letters' due to its flourishing literature and media traditions, Kottayam is nestled between the Western Ghats and the backwaters. As well as its cultural leanings, the town plays an important role in the spice and rubber trades. It's also a prominent hub for Kerala's Syrian Christian community, which has left a legacy of churches, chief among which are two St Mary's: Cheria Palli, the 'Little Church', and Valia Palli, the 'Big Church', both famous for their fabulous murals. The latter also boasts two granite Persian crosses.

Kottayam holds a couple of records that might please non-smoking bookworms: it was the first municipality in India to report a 100 per cent literacy rate and to declare itself totally non-smoking.

🔺 The kettuvallam *is the classic backwaters cruising vessel*

Vypin Island

There's so much to do in Kochi proper that few tourists make it over to Vypin (sometimes called Vypeen island), a short ferry ride north from Fort Kochin. It's a large island, 27 km (17 miles) long, and was created in 1341 by a heavy flood. Though it serves as a suburb to the city, and is by no means an undeveloped backwater, Vypin is distinct enough from its surroundings to provide a welcome change of pace from urban life, and the visitor will see plenty of traditional scenes here. There's probably not enough to detain you for more than a few hours, a day at the most, but the island does have a sprinkling of hotels, to cater to its nascent foreign tourism.

Vypin doesn't have must-see sights as such – though some of its more interesting attractions are listed below. The main fun consists in tootling around the island, appreciating the villagey ambience and enjoying some downtime. A good way to do this – owing to the isle's size – is by auto-rickshaw. You'll usually find some waiting at the jetty, and they are happy to negotiate a fee to take tourists to the main points of interest.

THINGS TO SEE & DO

Cherai Beach

Consisting of about 15 km (9 miles) of shoreline, you certainly won't go short of privacy here. And it is likely to be fishermen, cows and goats – plus the occasional naked male bather – who are your fellow beachgoers. Despite being near the city and a major shipping channel, the sea here is relatively clean, and it's possible to swim, though there is no lifeguard. Lagoons, set a little way back from the beach, add to the rustic charm.

Places of worship

From unexpected temples that are a riot of colour to imposing churches that seem more suited to a large city than an outlying island, Vypin's

⬤ *Collecting water, Vypin style*

religious sites are among its main landmarks. Local auto-rickshaw drivers will happily swing by the most interesting ones, of which Maha Vishnu and Sri Murigar temples, both near Cherai Beach, are two.

TAKING A BREAK

Tourist infrastructure is still in its infancy in Vypin, so if you're not staying in one of the few hotels on the island, your best bet for snacks and drinks are the small kiosks dotted around.

Munnar

Hill station Munnar is the town that tea built. It was developed by the British, who controlled the nearby tea plantations, some of the world's best. Though the town itself is shabby and unprepossessing, the wider area (Munnar can refer to either) contains some of Kerala's most incredible scenery. The neat rows of tea bushes that form the plantations themselves have an other-worldly quality to them, while the town's elevation – sitting at some 1,890 m (6,200 ft) it is Kerala's highest – ensures tremendous views.

Colonialism has also left a charming architectural legacy, in the British-built 1930s plantation bungalows. If your budget is elastic enough it is well worth shelling out to experience staying in one of these elegant homes, many of which contain authentic period furniture and offer the unique atmosphere of a bygone age. For more colonial reminiscing, the High Range Club (ⓦ www.highrangeclubmunnar.com), former rendezvous of the Raj-era chaps, is now open to non-members, but retains its men-only bar. Munnar is a handy base for exploration of some of the state's wildlife parks.

🔺 *Workers pick tea on Munnar's breathtaking plantations*

THINGS TO SEE & DO

Tata Tea Museum

It's all about the chai in Munnar. To learn more about the black stuff, head for this museum run by Tata, the big daddy of Indian industry. Historical equipment including a hundred-year-old roller, photographs and other colonial odds and ends are on display, and there is sometimes the opportunity to take part in some tea tasting.

ⓐ Nallathanni Estate, 1.5 km (1 mile) north of town centre ❶ (04865) 230 561 🕐 10.00–16.00 Tues–Sun, closed Mon ❶ Admission charge

TAKING A BREAK

If your stomach is game, a slew of stalls serving chapattis, puri and dosas line the main road.

Raspy Restaurant £ Basic market eatery, which supplements spicy Keralan staples such as parotta and biriyani with a few international options. For breakfast, try the shakshuka (a North African/Israeli egg dish) and chapatti. ⓐ Bazaar 🕐 06.30–21.30 daily

Hotel Saravan Bhavan £ Much-lauded South Indian cheap veggie eats served the old-school way on a banana leaf. The fast service and fine food means you may find yourself sharing a table. ⓐ Opposite Mount Carmel Church, near bus station ❶ (04865) 231 129 🕐 07.00–21.30 daily

AFTER DARK

Eastend Restaurant ££ One of Munnar's classier dining options is the restaurant at the Eastend resort. Wash down Chinese, continental, north and south Indian victuals with a decent bottle of wine or a coffee to the relaxing strains of classical music. There's also a separate café serving quick eats. ⓐ Temple Road ❶ (04865) 230 451 Ⓦ www.eastend.in ⓔ eastend@eastend.in

⬥ *Kerala's mountain country affords magnificent views*

Eravikulam National Park

Once a colonial hunting reserve for the British, this 97-sq-km (37-sq-miles) wilderness in the Western Ghats mountain range was declared a wildlife sanctuary in 1975 and accorded the status of a national park in 1978.

Serving as a haven for the rare Nilgiri tahr mountain goat, only a small section of this park – Rajamala – is open to the public. To enter the park you have to join a government tour bus, and visitors should head to Rajamala, from where the buses depart. The queues of people waiting to board can often be lengthy, but as foreign visitors are charged a significantly higher sum to enter the park they may be allowed to queue jump and you will probably be ushered onto the next bus. The tortuous journey into the park does not take too long, but the road up the hill winds its way alongside a sheer drop, so vertigo sufferers may prefer to look the other way (if they don't mind missing the tea plantation views!). Most Munnar resorts can arrange transport to the site.

Once at the park you can wander around and enjoy the wildlife and impressive views of mountains and tea crops. The goats don't seem particularly bothered by their endangered status, and allow humans to get up quite close. This is one reason why the park is so beloved of families – at weekends and holidays the bus rides can be rather busy – although if you are prepared to walk a bit you can shake off the crowds once in the park.

Tourist infrastructure here is rudimentary to say the least, and you're better off eating in Munnar before or afterwards.

ⓐ 16 km (10 m) north of Munnar Ⓦ www.eravikulam.org Ⓛ 07.00–18.00 daily (Sept–May) ❶ Admission charge

⬧ *Eravikulam National Park is home to the rare Nilgiri tahr mountain goat*

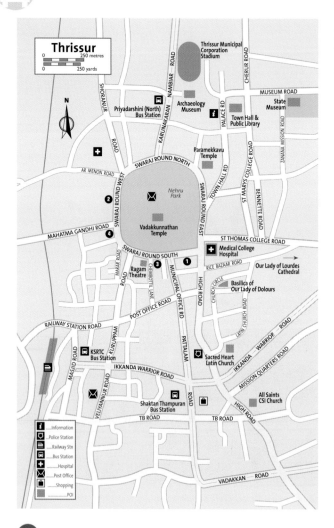

Thrissur

0 — 250 metres
0 — 250 yards

N

Thrissur Municipal
Corporation
Stadium

Archaeology
Museum

State
Museum

Priyadarshini (North)
Bus Station

Town Hall &
Public Library

Paramekkavu
Temple

Nehru
Park

Vadakkunnathan
Temple

ST THOMAS COLLEGE ROAD

Medical College
Hospital

Our Lady of Lourdes
Cathedral

Ragam
Theatre

Basilica of
Our Lady of Dolours

KSRTC
Bus Station

Sacred Heart
Latin Church

Shaktan Thampuran
Bus Station

All Saints
CSI Church

SHORANUR ROAD
NAMBIAR ROAD
KARUNAKARAN
CHERUR ROAD
MUSEUM ROAD
PALACE RD
AR MENON ROAD
SWARAJ ROUND NORTH
ZANANA MISSION ROAD
ST MARYS COLLEGE ROAD
TOWN HALL RD
SWARAJ ROUND WEST
SWARAJ ROUND EAST
BENNETTE ROAD
MAHATMA GANDHI ROAD
SWARAJ ROUND SOUTH
RICE BAZAAR ROAD
MARAR ROAD
CHEMBOTIL LANE
MUNICIPAL OFFICE RD
HIGH ROAD
CHURCH CIRCLE
LATIN CHURCH ROAD
POST OFFICE ROAD
RAILWAY STATION ROAD
MASJID ROAD
KURUPPAM
PATTALAM
IKKANDA WARRIOR ROAD
WARRIOR ROAD
VELIYANNUR ROAD
MISSION QUARTERS ROAD
HIGH ROAD
TB ROAD
TB ROAD
VADAKKAN ROAD

ℹ ...... Information
◉ ...... Police Station
🚉 ...... Railway Stn
🚌 ...... Bus Station
✚ ...... Hospital
✉ ...... Post Office
🏬 ...... Shopping
▬ ...... POI

Thrissur

Kerala's cultural capital is something of a festival-fest, the hub of many of the state's spiritual celebrations. It is here that the serious religious revelry goes down, and if you can time your visit to coincide with one of the many events – in particular the big one, the **Thrissur Pooram** (see page 106) – it will be an unforgettable spectacle. It follows that many of the top landmarks in Kerala's fourth-largest city are religious sites, be they Hindu, Christian or Muslim in denomination. The area is also a heartland for the state's art forms. But it's not all about piety and high-minded cultural pursuits. If you're after silks or gold, Thrissur also offers some of Kerala's top shopping.

THINGS TO SEE & DO

Religious sites

Thrissur's flagship sight is the imposing **Vadakkunnathan Temple**, an ancient edifice that sits proudly atop a hill, slap bang in the middle of town. Traditionally Keralan in design, it boasts an eye-catching pagoda-style roof, detailed woodcarvings and eye-catching murals. To get inside, non-Hindus need to go in April, during the Thrissur Pooram (see page 106). But even at other times the splendid exterior can be enjoyed.
ⓐ Centre of town ⓣ (0487) 242 6040 ⓛ 04.30–11.00 & 17.00–20.30 daily
ⓘ Apr only for non-Hindus

The spectacular **Our Lady of Lourdes Cathedral**, with its bright white European-influenced frontage and soaring spires, rivals Vadakkunnathan aesthetically.
ⓐ East Fort ⓣ (0487) 233 3995 ⓦ www.lourdescathedralthrissur.com
ⓔ mail@lourdescathedralthrissur.com ⓛ 06.30–18.30 daily

Asia's biggest and tallest church, the Indo-Gothic **Basilica of Our Lady of Dolours**, or Puthan Pally/Puttanpalli, is a riot of colour inside, with dazzling altars, excellent murals and Biblical scenes. Several other temples, churches and mosques can be found in and around the town if your appetite is whetted.

⬣ *Our Lady of Lourdes Cathedral is one of Thrissur's architectural gems*

ⓐ East of High Road ⓣ (0487) 242 0906 ⓦ www.doloursbasilica.com
ⓔ mail@doloursbasilica.com ⓛ 08.15–20.15 daily

TAKING A BREAK

Indian Coffee House £ ❶ Kerala's famous coffee cooperative started
life in Thrissur, so a visit to the local branch will have a historical as well
as a refreshment element. There is another outlet on Railway Station
Road. ⓐ Swaraj Round South ⓣ (0487) 326 0222 ⓛ 07.00–21.30

AFTER DARK

Ambady Restaurant £ ❷ With some outdoor seating, Ambady does a
roaring trade serving set-menu South Indian cuisine to local families.
ⓐ 25/900 Swaraj Round West ⓣ (0487) 233 5770 ⓛ 10.00–23.00 (approx)

Ming Palace £ ❸ If you're suffering from curry fatigue, go
gastronomically eastwards to Ming Palace, a Chinese worthy of the
name which even comes with red lanterns. The Chinese and Thai dishes
here are decent enough and the prices reasonable. ⓐ Pathans Building,
second floor, Swaraj Round South, near Ragam Theatre ⓣ (0487) 242 8823
ⓛ 11.00–22.00 daily

Navaratna Restaurant £ ❹ Diner-style booths add to the sophisticated
ambience here, where vegetarians are particularly well catered for with
North Indian standards. ⓐ Naduvilal, Swaraj Round West ⓣ (0487) 242
1994 ⓛ 10.00–23.00 daily

Wayanad

Nestled high up in the Western Ghats, stunning Wayanad is a gateway to a bygone India. Populated still by nomadic tribes, the area's lifeblood is agriculture. Coffee is the big one, but the tea, cocoa, pepper, plantain, rice, rubber and vanilla that are also grown are responsible for the idyllic, misty plantation scenes that call to mind an Indian Shangri-La. Dense, virgin forests add to the allure. It follows that many of Wayanad's attractions are of the natural variety, and the wildlife that its relative seclusion offers are indeed a big draw. But humanity too has left its mark on the district, and the cultural stops are also well worth making.

THINGS TO SEE & DO

Edakkal Caves

Ancient rock engravings – the oldest of which date back a staggering 8,000 years – and awe-inspiring views repay the lengthy climb to these two caves, if you have the energy for it.

ⓐ Near Ambalavayal ⏱ 09.00–17.00 daily ⓘ Admission charge

Jain Temple

Believed to date from the 13th century, the temple served the Jains, devotees of an ancient Indian religion that prescribed non-violence and pursuing divine consciousness. The building is in pretty good shape considering its age, and its pillars ring with a sense of history and majesty. The beautiful stone carvings are a highlight.

ⓐ Near Sultan Battery ⏱ 08.00–12.00 & 14.00–18.00 daily

Wayanad Wildlife Sanctuary

Part of the Nilgiri Biosphere Reserve, a protected area that is under consideration as a UNESCO World Heritage Site, the 345-sq-km (133-sq-mile) Wayanard sanctuary is home to safari favourites such as the elephant, tiger, panther, monkey, Indian bison, deer and peacock. The park

⬧ *Dense forest characterises the elevated district of Wayanad*

cannot be toured independently. Visitors, who remain few in number despite the park's obvious attractions, must rent a jeep and travel with a guide, though guided walks are possible during set times and in set areas. Naturally, visitors go to see the animals, but the splendid landscape, with its teak forests, rugged terrain, mountain backdrops and pretty watering holes is adequate compensation if the wildlife is feeling shy. Logistical help and information is available from the local District Tourism Promotion Council (ⓐ Kalpetta ⓣ (0471) 232 1132 ⓦ www.dtpcwayanad.com).

ⓐ 16 km (10 km) east of Sultan Battery on road to Mysore
ⓛ 07.00–17.00 daily ⓘ Admission charge

ⓞ *A wooden statue of Ganesh in Kollam*

LIFESTYLE
Keralan life

Food and drink

Diversity – in religion, culture and geography – is the lynchpin of Kerala's gastronomy. Many Indians will tell the visitor that the idea of 'Indian food' as a homogenous concept is a nonsense, because cuisine differs so much from state to state and region to region. This is true to an extent, although there's still plenty of the firm favourites: curry, dosa, tandoori, biriyani, naan, idli and, of course, an abundance of spice.

Cultural melting pot

Keralan cuisine reflects the various cultures that have left their mark on the state. Before Kerala itself was created, the area was made up of the states of Malabar in the north, with its predominantly non-vegetarian fare, and the vegetarian enclaves of Travancore and Kochi – the two princely states to the south. Having three large religious communities has also conferred variety on local eating habits. A surfeit of bakeries bears testimony to European settlers, while potatoes, tomatoes and chillies are the legacy of the Americas. The ultra-cosmopolitan Kochi, with its Portuguese, Dutch, British and Jewish connections, generates even more of a smorgasbord, and should be a first stop for any visiting foodie.

Keralan staples

The state's name – said to be a rough fusion of *kera* (meaning 'coconut tree') and *alam* ('land') – contains a clue to one of Kerala's main food sources. Grated coconut and coconut milk crop up constantly, used both for consistency and taste. The other two members of the Keralan food trio are bananas, bunches of which can be seen hanging in nearly every market, and tapioca. The coastal towns have access to a wealth of seafood, and you can often see that night's dinner being hauled out of the sea earlier in the day – great for both food miles and freshness.

At the heart of the meal is rice, which in Kerala generally comes pre-boiled, with the grain cooked in its husk, lending the dish a flecked appearance. It is usually served with vegetable or curry accompaniments (in the plural), with the addition of meat for omnivores.

Vegetarian food

Kerala's large Hindu contingent means that, unlike in much of the developing world, vegetarians are well catered for. The more basic restaurants even divide their menus, so there is no chance of the committed veggie accidentally ingesting any unidentifiable meat substance.

Spices

Macho fans of blazing curries will be pleased to know that Keralan food is as hot as its national identity, but chefs can usually tone down the spices a few notches to suit more delicate European palates. Garlic is a common flavouring, as are cardamom, cinnamon, cloves, coriander, cumin, ginger, peppers and turmeric.

🔻 *A coconut seller takes a rest by his merchandise at a Kollam market*

Ayurvedic food

One spice-free (and meat-free) area is Ayurvedic cuisine, which you'll get to sample if you spend any time in a dedicated resort or restaurant. The thinking behind the diet is extensive, but the basic idea is finding out what your *dosha* (constitution) is and then eating the correct foods (drawn from the six different tastes) to keep it balanced. While Ayurveda holds that anything can be a food, meat or poison depending on the individual circumstances, the general principles advocate eating fresh, seasonal, light, simple, mild food, in response to hunger. For those sensitive to spices, Ayurvedic eating can be a refreshingly easy-going respite.

Drinks

The chai or coffee wallah is never far away in Kerala. Tea comes with milk and sugar, coffee usually black, although the better establishments will allow you to specify how you want it. Fresh lime juice with soda is ubiquitous – and a welcome refresher in hot weather. Coconut juice, unsurprisingly, is also widely available. The coconut palm is also the source of the state wine known, from British days, as the toddy, a boozy drink that should only be sampled by the robust of constitution. Toddy shops often serve as social hubs for local men.

Sweets and desserts

Milk is the main ingredient of many Keralan desserts. You'll find it in *payasam*, the most popular pudding, which also contains coconut

ALCOHOLIC DRINKS

Note that strict alcohol sale laws mean that many smaller establishments are not permitted to serve drink. While many establishments, especially in the larger towns, obey, others get around the edict by various tricks such as serving beer in opaque mugs or getting customers to keep their bottles on the floor rather than the table. If you find yourself craving a drink, the more upmarket places have usually shelled out for a licence.

extract, sugar, cashews and dry grapes. Banana-based *pradhamam* is another favourite, and the fruit is also enjoyed in bread and dried form, as well as on its own. Mangoes are delicious when in season, during the summer. Coconuts, guavas, jackfruit, pineapples and papayas are also seasonally available. Keralans tend to take sweets as a snack, rather than to round off a meal.

Where to eat

From swanky restaurants to street stalls, the main resorts afford plenty of choice for culinary venues. At the upper end of the scale are fine dining establishments, usually in top hotels, that make full use of Kerala's coast and Indian flavours to bring you a delectable banquet of a meal. But an equally interesting gastronomic experience can be had in local 'meals' restaurants, where for a fixed sum you can enjoy a hearty and traditional Keralan feast. Canny restaurateurs have their eye on foreign tourists, and most eateries in the resorts also serve 'continental' or 'European' food – typically pasta, pizza and a few meat-based standards. In the northern, less touristy parts, expect a great deal less choice of where and what to eat.

When to eat

Traditionally a farming, fishing state, Keralans don't stay up that late and outside Kochi it's difficult to find anywhere to eat much after 10pm. Most eateries in the resorts are open all day, serving breakfast from around 8am. Hotels will have more specific meal times.

Any menu presented to a tourist is certain to have an English translation (the truly local locals don't deal in menus anyway). However, Keralans are always appreciative of visitors' attempts – no matter how faltering – to speak in Malayalam.

Menu decoder

POPULAR DISHES

Ada pradhaman Milk-based jaggery dessert

Aviyal Thick mixture of a lot vegetables, curd and coconut

Biryani Spicy rice dish with meat or vegetables, saffron or turmeric

Chakka pradhaman Jaggery-based paste pudding

Dal Pulses, or pulse stew

Dosa South Indian crepe made with rice and black lentils

Idli South Indian savoury cake made of fermented black lentils and rice

Injipuli Dark curry with ginger, green chillies and jaggery, sometimes known as puli inji

Kaalan Thick yoghurt, coconut and vegetable dish

Kanji Rice porridge

Masala A blend of spices, typically black pepper, cardamom, cinnamon, cloves, coriander, nutmeg, and turmeric

Meen mulakittathu Spicy red fish curry with a thin sauce

Meen pathiri Steamed rice with fish masala

Meen pollichathu Roasted fish in a banana leaf wrap

Meen varattiyathu Fish curry in a thick coconut sauce

Mouli Fish curry with coconut milk

Naichoru Biryani from the northern Malabar region

Olan Pumpkin, coconut milk and ginger seasoned with coconut oil.

Pathiri Rice chapattis served with meat dishes

Payasam Sweet milk dish with rice or vermicelli

Puttu Steamed rice cakes

Rasam Spicy South Indian vegetable and lentil soup

Sadya Traditional vegetarian banquet served with boiled rice and side-dishes on a banana leaf, often on special occasions

Sambar South Indian vegetable stew or chowder

Tandoori Food cooked in a cylindrical clay oven
Thheyal Spicy roasted coconut dish similar to sambar
Thoran Dry dish of grated coconut
Uperi Dried banana or vegetable

FOOD STAPLES

Annam, ari, choru Rice
Ays Ice
Caaya Tea
Brinjal, vazhuthananga Aubergine
Ethapazham, pazham Banana
Etheka, nendrakka Plantain
Irachi Meat
Kaapi Coffee
Karimeen Pearlspot fish
Kasuvandipparippu Cashew nut
Kodampuli Keralan tamarind
Kolli, kappa, marichini, poolakizhaghu Tapioca
Kolikkari Chicken
Kurumulaku Black pepper
Manga, mampalam Mango
Matthanga Pumpkin
Meen Fish
Mulaku Chilli

Muringakkaya Drumstick
Musambi Sweet lime
Mutta Egg
Nalikeram, thenga Coconut
Paal, palu Milk
Palam Fruit
Panjasara Sugar
Puli Tamarind
Roti Bread
Sasyam, paccakkri Vegetables
Tairu Yoghurt, curd
Thakkali Tomato
Ulli, savala, sabola Onion
Uppu Salt
Urulakkizhangu Potato
Velichenna Coconut oil
Vellam Water
Vendakka Okra
Venna Butter

AT THE RESTAURANT

Dayavaai Please
E vellam kudikkan kollamo? Is this water safe to drink?
Ente bill tharoo/tharumo Can I have the bill please?
Kutikkuka To drink
Mulaku illa Without chilli
Nan venam... I would like...
Nanni Thank you
Tailet evide? Where is the toilet?

Shopping

Kerala might not be quite the shopper's delight that Goa is, but there are still plenty of tempting bargains with which to fill your suitcase on your return journey. Chief among them are the beautiful – and easily transportable – fabrics. Whether it's hippie clothes, a sari, a silk, a throw or a bag, a dazzling array of bright colours and styles are on offer, and such items have a big fashion cachet back in the West. Many of the items on sale can be found elsewhere in India, so if you want to stay strictly Keralan about it, the best choice is the *kasavu*, an off-white sari with a gold border.

The state's ubiquitous coconut trees serve as a source for a lot of the local merchandise. *Coir*, made from coconut fibre, is fashioned into mats, bags, wall hangings and even coasters. The hub of the industry, Alappuzha, is a good place to start. Other quirky handicrafts include masks, woodcarvings, weavings and musical instruments. Elephants tend to pop up quite a lot, as ornaments and on bags and fabrics, as do multi-armed Hindu deities, who make bright and cheerful paintings. Intricate jewellery and gold are on sale, often by weight, but don't expect the bargain-basement prices you might find with other products.

Edibles are another good gift choice. Cashews are big in Kerala, while banana chips are also a popular snack. The staples of spices and tea are quintessential Indian buys and also convenient for transporting home.

The state's main shopping hubs are its big cities. In Trivandrum the retail action centres on MG Road and to a lesser extent Powerhouse Road and Chalai Bazaar. In Kochi, MG Road is again the place to shop, and there is also a concentration of tourist-orientated outlets in Jew Town, although the hassle factor can be high. The same is true of the seafront at Kovalam, where persistent traders stalk the restaurants. Wherever you end up, a sensible place to head for to avoid being hustled is the government emporium (called Kairali in Kochi and Calicut and SMSM Handicrafts in Trivandrum). Failing that, the less touristy areas generally offer the greatest chances of paying a fair price and avoiding the hard sell.

In most places, though, you will have to haggle. How mercenary you want to be is a personal choice – some visitors don't mind paying a bit over the odds because of the big income disparity between buyer and seller – but bear in mind that the first price you are quoted may be several times what the vendor would be prepared to accept.

Another fascinating shopping experience – though one where you might not want to buy anything – is the local market, where oddities ranging from weird spices to severed animal parts are on show. Probably not the image the government is aiming to promote through its Grand Kerala Shopping Festival, a 45-day retail-fest at the end of the year (www.grandkeralashoppingfestival.com).

⬤ *A head for business: a roving vendor transports his fabrics around Kovalam*

Children

Keralans are warm and welcoming to all tourists, and that coupled with the child-friendliness of Indian society at large makes the state a hospitable destination to bring your brood. While it might not be the most obvious destination for a family holiday, Kerala still boasts a wealth of attractions for younger visitors. Chief among them are the simple

🔺 *India is a famously child-friendly society*

pleasures of the beach: paddling, splashing around and sandcastle construction. Nearby stalls or shops can usually furnish you with a bucket and spade, beach ball and the like.

The state's wildlife will also delight children. The tigers and elephants of Periyar always cause excitement, and you can sometimes get up quite close, as with Eravikulam's rare goats (see page 84). The thrill of hearing a herd of deer thunder past just metres away will be a lasting memory. But even if you don't plan your trip around fauna, there will be plenty of other pleasant surprises from the natural world, such as Kerala's 300 or more types of gorgeous butterfly and nearly 500 species of bird.

If you're travelling with older children, taking in a *kathakali* dance-drama show will be an unforgettable evening. Things usually start with a series of comical facial expressions that kids will enjoy, but the main event is the acting out of a melodramatic story by characters in such OTT costumes and make-up that they make a pantomime dame seem low key by comparison. The plots can be macabre and proceedings do get quite loud, so *kathakali* might not suit very young or easily spooked children.

Aside from Kerala-specific attractions, you also have the vivid panorama of India to occupy young visitors. Hurtling along in an auto-rickshaw may not be most adults' idea of fun, but children will love the novelty. The incessant brightness and colour – in the extravagant saris, bustling markets and brilliant temples with their many-limbed gods – make a vivid backdrop that will transfix children used to orderly, western cities. Another advantage to travel in India is the relatively low cost of most things. This can allow you to buy a greater level of comfort and security more suited to a family – hiring a car and a driver rather than subjecting your offspring to a bumpy bus ride, for example.

For a smooth holiday, you will need to take some precautions. The main travel risks of India – stomach upsets from unsafe water or spicy food, the heat, chaotic traffic and stray animals – apply even more so to unwary children. The state's child-friendliness doesn't translate into a lot of provisions for kids, so you can't assume you will find highchairs, children's menus and so on. You will also need to bring disposable nappies with you.

Sports & activities

The state's varied geography and rich culture ensures no shortage of things to do – your biggest problem will probably be prioritising your activities on a limited trip. From the beaches to the backwaters, the mountains to the metropolises, Kerala will keep you thoroughly occupied and entertained.

Ayurveda and yoga

Well-being junkies will want to get their fix of India's traditional healing system. How deep you go is up to the individual. To do it by the book, you would undertake a course of treatment of a week or longer, involving medical consultations, massage with oils, meditation and herbal remedies, sometimes with some yoga thrown in for good measure. Retreats such as **Nilayoram** (Ⓦ www.ayurvedakerala.biz), outside Thrissur, offer dedicated packages. But most holidaymakers just dabble with the odd relaxing massage or hour of yoga.

Watersports and boat trips

Given the large amount of water in or off Kerala, aquatic pursuits are likely to feature in your trip to some degree. The state doesn't have the thriving and organised watersports scene that you would find in more touristy places like Goa – a good thing for its peace and tranquillity, some would say – but Kerala's beaches do afford opportunities to get wet and wild if that's your cup of tea. Canoeing, catamaran sailing, kayaking, parasailing, scuba diving, snorkelling and windsurfing are all possible. But the main water-based fun is had cruising the backwaters, a topic covered in more detail on pages 76 & 78. If you want to hit the high seas, local fisherman are sometimes willing to take tourists out in their boats for a small cash sum.

Kathakali and evening entertainment

Kerala's nightlife – what there is of it – is laid back and low key. It's possible to while away a pleasant evening in the resorts of Kovalam and Varkala, as well as Kochi, although the state's strict alcohol laws preclude much of a party vibe. When the sun goes down, a fun option is to take in a *kathakali* performance. The local dance-dramas are riotous pantomimes set to music, where fabulously made-up and costumed actors stage eye-popping melodramas. Fort Kochi has two venues, the Kerala *Kathakali* Centre (W www.kathakalicentre.com), which stages a daily show at 18.00, and the Kochi Cultural Centre (W www.kochiculturalcentre.com), whose performance takes place at 18.30.

Nature and wildlife

Nature lovers will be in their element in Kerala, whose lush greenery provides refuge for a wealth of wildlife. The state is rich in nature reserves, of which the most famous is Periyar, where elephants and occasionally tigers can be spotted. Even when the animals prove elusive, these areas are home to some fantastic scenery. But there's plenty of nature to enjoy even without making a special journey – outside the dedicated zones, you're bound to come across butterflies and birds galore.

⬤ *Take a dip in the Brunton Boatyard Hotel pool, overlooking Kochi's harbour*

Festivals and events

Kerala is colourful enough on the average day, but festivals here take it to another level. Many of the celebrations are linked to the Hindu religion. Elephants tend to play quite a major role, to the chagrin of animal rights activists who bemoan the harsh conditions in which they are kept the rest of the time. The main festivals are listed here, but check locally when you arrive, to find out if something is going to be held during your stay.

JANUARY–MARCH
Ernakulathappan Temple Utsavam
The raising of the temple flag signals the beginning of eight days of traditional music and dance, fireworks, shopping and other religious fun. As is often the case in Kerala, the elephants also get a run out, with 15 of them parading on the seventh day. ⓐ Shiva Temple, Ernakulam, Kochi ⓛ Jan–Feb

Malabar Mahotsavam
This cultural festival showcases classical music and dance, traditional folk and arts, drama, literature and more. With all events free of charge, the aim is to make the Southern Indian region of Malabar's performing arts accessible to all as well as attract tourists and culture vultures from India and beyond. ⓐ Calicut ⓛ 13–16 Jan

APRIL–JUNE
Thrissur Pooram
This elephantine extravaganza is known as 'the pooram of all poorams' (temple festivals). As many as a hundred of the ornately decorated creatures in fancy headdresses parade through the cultural capital of Thrissur with much accompanying pomp and circumstance – trumpet playing, drum beating and cymbal clashing. The 36-hour spectacular ends in a firework display. ⓐ Thrissur ⓛ mid-April–mid-May

Vishu

The first day of the first month of the Malayalam calendar is believed to be a harbinger of the year ahead. A family affair, the day involves making *kani* from coconut, fruit, cereals and flowers. Blindfolded children are led to the *kani* where they are blessed and given money by the family elders. ⏱ Apr–May

JULY–SEPTEMBER

Independence Day of India

Keralans join in with the nationwide celebrations of the moment that India gained independence from the British in 1947 and was born as a sovereign nation. Parades, flag-hoisting, speeches and patriotic fervour mark the occasion, which is a national holiday. ⓐ Across the country ⏱ 15 Aug

Navratri

Literally meaning 'nine nights', this Hindu festival of worship and dance is celebrated in Trivandrum, and other places around the state, with a music festival. ⏱ Sept–Oct

Nehru Trophy Boat Race

Keralans make good use of their state's vast expanse of water by racing on it, and of all the competitions, this is the biggie. Huge canoes up to 37 m (120 ft) long, known as snake boats and sometimes seating over a hundred oarsmen, do aquatic battle for the much-coveted replica silver snake boat trophy. The event has been going since 1952, when independent India's first prime minister visited Kerala and enjoyed his ride in a snake boat so much that he donated a trophy for the locals to race for. ⓐ Punnamada Lake, Alappuzha ⓦ www.nehrutrophy.nic.in ⏱ second Saturday in Aug

Onam

Held to commemorate the homecoming of the celebrated King Mahabali, who was banished by the gods for his self-centredness, but

LIFESTYLE

permitted to return once a year to greet his former subjects. The Onam carnival, a harvest festival, is the state's biggest. Snake boat racing, *kaikottikali* folk-dancing, a nine-course feast, game-playing and various decorations and clothes all feature in ten days of celebrations.
Ⓦ www.onamfestival.org Ⓛ Aug–Sept

OCTOBER–JANUARY
Christmas & New Year
Kerala's Christians might represent less than a fifth of the state's population, but that doesn't mean that the religion's main festivals go by unheeded. Members of the Syrian Orthodox denomination (who constitute the majority of the state's Christian contingent) do not swap presents. The fireworks, processions and hymns that celebrate the occasion are all very much Indian in spirit. Christmas trees are a very recent advent and still rare. To ring in the New Year, Kochi hosts a week's worth of games, masquerade dances and competitions which culminate in a colourful, costume-packed, Portuguese-influenced procession on New Year's Day. Ⓛ 25 Dec; 1 Jan

Sabarimala festival
High up in the Western Ghats, this festival centres on the pilgrimage that devotees from India and overseas make to the famous Sabarimala Sri Dharmasastha Temple. Parashurama, a warrior incarnation of Vishnu, who legend has it created Kerala by throwing his axe, is said to have installed an idol at this temple himself, so the pilgrimage is a very serious business. Strict conditions govern participation (wearing black, vegetarianism and abstaining from carnal pleasures for 41 days are required, and women of child-bearing age are banned totally). Up to 200,000 attend. Pilgrimage season lasts for three months but the actual journey takes a week. Ⓛ Nov–Jan Ⓦ www.sabarimala.org

Ⓓ *Rooms on stilts enjoy a pool view at the Ramada Resort, Kochi*

 # PRACTICAL INFORMATION
Tips & advice

Accommodation

The following price ratings are based on a double room with breakfast in high season for one night. (AC = air conditioning)

£ = up to Rs 1,000   **££** = Rs 1,000-5,000   **£££** = over Rs 5,000

BACKWATERS

Oberoi Vrinda £££ The Vrinda offers Keralan cruising in style. Service, accommodation and food are all second to none. Daily excursions and entertainment. ⓐ Departs from Vembanad Lake ⓣ (0484) 266 9595 ⓦ www.oberoihotels.com

CALICUT

Alakapuri £ Close to the major transport links, this quiet option enjoys a touch of old-world glamour. Its cottages, AC and non-AC rooms will not eat into your holiday budget too much. ⓐ Moulana Mohammed Ali Road ⓣ (0495) 272 3451 ⓦ www.alakapurihotels.com

KANNUR

Government Guest House £ Sea views and great value for money recommend this state-run option. Decent, spacious rooms, some with balconies and AC. ⓐ By Sea View Park ⓣ (0497) 270 6426

KASARAGOD

Gitanjali Heritage ££ This heritage homestay tries to gives its guests the Keralan cultural experience. The same company also operates a houseboat on the lesser-known northern backwaters. ⓐ Panayal, Kasaragod ⓣ (0467) 223 4159 ⓦ www.gitanjaliheritage.com

Oyster Opera ££ Part-theme village, part-resort, part-working fish farm, quirky Oyster Opera enjoys a serene location surrounded by water and palm trees. Seafood lovers will be in their element – mussels and oysters are brought fresh to your table. ⓐ Thekkekadu, Padanna Kadapuram, Kasaragod ⓣ 944 717 6465 ⓦ www.oysteroperaatpadanna.com

KOCHI

Ramada Resort ££/£££ This relaxing resort-style hotel lies slightly outside the city. The high-tech rooms, built on stilts, ooze style and class.
ⓐ Kumbalam South ⓣ (0484) 301 1100 Ⓦ www.ramadacochin.com

Brunton Boatyard £££ Atmospheric heritage hotel in the heart of Fort Kochi. An emphasis on history and the environment make this a great choice for the ethical and culturally minded traveller. ⓐ 1/498 Fort Kochi
ⓣ (0484) 301 1711 Ⓦ www.cghearth.com

KOVALAM

Hotel Sea Breeze £ It's very basic, but Sea Breeze has large balconies, AC and non-AC rooms and is just a few minutes' walk from the beach.
ⓐ Just off Lighthouse Beach ⓣ 984 733 0800 Ⓦ www.edakkad.in

Leela £££ Cream-of-the-crop option that offers all the luxuries, attention to detail and service that you would expect from the exclusive Leela chain. ⓐ North of Hawah Beach ⓣ (0471) 248 0101 Ⓦ www.theleela.com

MUZHAPPILANGAD

Edakkad Beach Houses ££ Simple, seaside accommodation in a couple of houses set among the trees. This is true off-the-beaten-track territory.
ⓐ North of Muzhappilangad Beach ⓣ 984 733 0800 Ⓦ www.edakkad.in

TRIVANDRUM

Hotel Regency £ Centrally located yet quiet, this friendly place offers AC and non-AC rooms with satellite TV. ⓐ Manjalikulam Cross Road, Thampanoor ⓣ (0471) 233 0377 Ⓦ www.hotelregency.com

VARKALA

Krishnatheeram ££ Simple and rustic cottages, with all mod cons, in a serene setting close to the beach. Ayurveda and yoga are also on offer.
ⓐ Thiruvambadi (Black) Beach ⓣ (0470) 260 1305
Ⓦ www.krishnatheeram.in

 PRACTICAL INFORMATION

Preparing to go

GETTING THERE

Some package holidays to Kerala do exist, but there is not yet the range
of options that you would find for Goa. Some scheduled airlines, such as
Air India, Emirates, Gulf Air, Qatar Airways and SriLankan Airlines fly to
Kerala via their respective hubs. Fares start from around £500.

Air India Ⓦ www.airindia.com
Emirates Ⓦ www.emirates.com
Gulf Air Ⓦ www.gulfair.com
Qatar Airways Ⓦ www.qatarairways.com
SriLankan Airlines Ⓦ www.srilankan.aero

If you're travelling within India, you can take an internal flight to one
of the state's three airports, Trivandrum, Kochi and Calicut. The majority
of international destinations out of Kerala's airports are Asian or Middle
Eastern, although Monarch does operate seasonal flights to the state.
The domestic airlines all have useful websites for finding out times and
fares, but not all of them accept international credit cards for online
bookings so you may have to book with a local travel agent upon
arrival in India. Prices are usually reasonable, particularly if you book well
in advance.

The country's domestic airlines are listed below:

Air India Express Ⓦ www.airindiaexpress.in
GoAir Ⓦ www.goair.in
Indian Airlines Ⓦ indian-airlines.nic.in
IndiGo Ⓦ www.goindigo.in
Jet Airways Ⓦ www.jetairways.com
Jet Lite Ⓦ www.jetlite.com
Kingfisher Airlines Ⓦ www.flykingfisher.com
Paramount Airways Ⓦ www.paramountairways.com
Spice Jet Ⓦ www.spicejet.com

Many people are aware that air travel emits CO_2, which contributes
to climate change. You may be interested in the possibility of lessening
the environmental impact of your flight through the charity Climate

Care, which offsets your CO_2 by funding environmental projects around the world. Visit Ⓦ www.jpmorganclimatecare.com

A more colourful and even cheaper way to reach Kerala is by train. It is certainly taking the scenic route – the distances and speeds mean that some journeys can be seriously long – but India has some glorious railway voyages if you have the patience for the duration, lack of luxury and vagaries of the seating reservation system. The railway network website has full details of the timetable (Ⓦ www.indianrail.gov.in).

TOURISM AUTHORITY

The Kerala Tourism Development Corporation has a network of hotels and resorts (from budget to expensive) and it also runs tours: (Ⓦ www.ktdc.com).

The state Department of Tourism also has a useful website: (Ⓦ www.keralatourism.org).

BEFORE YOU LEAVE

Take medical advice six weeks before your trip, in case you need a course of inoculations. Diphtheria, tetanus and polio vaccinations are recommended for travel to India, and you may also want to consider inoculation against hepatitis A, hepatitis B, typhoid and meningitis. Kerala is considered a low-risk area for malaria, but advice on the need for anti-malarial tablets varies – consult your doctor.

TRAVEL INSURANCE

Taking out travel insurance is strongly recommended. The most basic packages start from around £2 a day for a two-week break. If you travel frequently, an annual multi-trip policy can work out better value. If you do go for a basic package, you may not be covered for activities such as some watersports, so bear this in mind before you choose

While you shouldn't have any problem picking up essentials like suntan lotion in the major towns, if you're going off the beaten track or if you take anything specific, such as the contraceptive pill, it's worth bringing enough to cover you for your trip. A first-aid kit could also be an idea if you are visiting remoter spots or travelling with children.

ENTRY REQUIREMENTS

It comes as a surprise to many, but all foreigners need to get a visa before coming to India. The usual one given to tourists is the six-month, multiple-entry visa, even if you're only coming once and staying for two weeks. Apply at your nearest Indian embassy. In the UK the visa application system has been outsourced. Apply online, by post or in person in London; there are also centres in Birmingham and Edinburgh. The processing time is typically two to three working days but it can be longer at busier periods. Your travel agent may also be able to take care of it. Passports must be valid for at least six months after your stay.

Customs declaration forms are handed out on the plane to India. You're entitled to import a litre each of wine and spirits and 200 cigarettes or the equivalent.

MONEY

India's currency is the rupee. The law forbids the import (and export) of rupees, but is seldom enforced. The larger towns have plenty of reliable ATMs and bureaux de change, though changing money can be rather bureaucratic. Credit cards are accepted at the more upmarket establishments, but guesthouses and restaurants are not likely to take cards.

CLIMATE

Peak season in Kerala is from the end of November to March, coinciding with European and North American winter. For these months it is warm without being sweltering and relatively dry. From April to June, the temperature soars to above 40°C (104°F), which is very hard going for travellers. That period is brought to an end by the southwest monsoon, which lasts from the middle of June to October and gives way to the supposedly milder northeast monsoon, which runs through to December. The state's lush greenery is no accident – Kerala gets a lot of rain, which can often be torrential. If you're not in the state for a sunshine break – or trying to get anywhere – the rain can be rather picturesque. Indeed, some people who are in Kerala for non-beach reasons – a stay at an Ayurveda resort for example – deliberately time their visit for the monsoon for the atmosphere, and also because of the large discounts available for those travelling outside peak season.

Temperature-wise, things vary a lot by elevation. While the coastal areas stay warm for pretty much the whole year, head up into the Western Ghats and it's quite a different matter. Hill stations are much chillier whenever you visit, and in the cooler months can hover just a few degrees above zero.

BAGGAGE ALLOWANCE

How much luggage your airline will allow and in what permutations varies with the airport, carrier, political events, policy shifts and much else. Generally, scheduled airlines are more generous than their low-cost counterparts and charter flights, allowing around 20 kg. Most airline websites have a section on the current allowance, or you can check with your travel agent if you've booked a package holiday.

● *Some of your Keralan sojourn is likely to be spent on water*

During your stay

AIRPORTS

Kerala has three airports, which are – in order of busyness – Kochi, Trivandrum and Calicut. Kochi's modern hub is in Nedumbassery, about 30 km (19 miles) northeast of the city. A taxi ride into town should be in the region of £6 to £9 and in heavy traffic can take as long as an hour and a half. Trivandrum is just 6 km (3¾ miles) from the city. There's a prepaid taxi stand, where you'll pay just over £2.50 to get into town. You can also take the number 14 bus (although it probably won't display its number). Fewer tourists pass through Calicut airport, which is in Karipur, 23 km (14 miles) from the town, but should you pitch up there it does have a prepaid taxi kiosk.

COMMUNICATIONS

If you find yourself without a mobile, and needing to make a call from Kerala, look out for the small booths displaying the letters PCO/STD/ISD. Any type of calls can be made from these places, which are sometimes open 24 hours, with the charge usually coming up on a meter. This is

Telephoning Kerala
From the UK 00 + 91 + area code + number
From Ireland 00 + 91 + area code + number
From the US 011 + 91 + area code + number
From Canada 011 + 91 + area code + number

Telephoning abroad
The UK 00 + 44 + number
Ireland 00 + 353 + number
The US 00 + 1 + number
Canada 00 + 1 + number

Dial 197 for Directory Enquiries.

likely to be much cheaper than calling from your hotel, especially if it's an upmarket one.

However, most travellers these days make do with their mobiles. Unless you're on an extended trip or need to make and receive a high number of calls, when it can be more economical to invest in an Indian SIM card, your home mobile should suffice. Various networks (including Airtel, Vodafone and Idea) cover the state; in the major resorts coverage is good, but you may lose reception in the remoter areas.

As a rapidly growing market of over a billion people, Indian telephone numbers tend to change quite frequently, often without much warning. The authorities are trying to standardise them to ten digits (without the 0), including the area code. If you're vainly attempting to get through to a number that has fewer, try adding a 2 to the number itself.

The Indian postal service works well for simple undertakings like sending postcards but if you want to dispatch a parcel expect reams of red tape. It costs Rs 12 to send a postcard overseas and Rs 20 a letter. Hotels often sell stamps along with postcards. Stick the stamps on before writing the cards, as multiple ones are sometimes required, obliterating your weather and activity report. Postboxes, which tend to vaguely resemble British ones, are easily recognisable, though it can be safer to hand in your completed cards at the post office itself.

The internet has taken off in a big way in India. In all but the furthest-flung reaches of the state you'll find internet cafés aplenty. Growing numbers of hotels now provide WiFi access, and even where coverage is limited it is sometimes possible to get hooked up via a USB dial-up modem, although that can be slow and troublesome.

CUSTOMS

Saying 'namaskaram' with your palms together (as if you were praying) is the traditional state salutation, and Keralans are usually delighted if a foreigner greets them in this way. Most people appreciate a handshake, although more conservative women might feel awkward about shaking hands with a man, so it's better to let the woman initiate it. And make sure it's your right hand both for shaking and eating – in Indian culture

the left hand is used for cleaning up after the toilet and therefore considered unclean.

Point with your entire hand rather than one finger, and try not to expose the soles of your feet to anyone as it is considered offensive. Overt displays of affection are also taboo. While most Keralans are willing – sometimes outright enthusiastic – to be photographed, it's better to check first.

The legendary Indian head wobble has perplexed outsiders for generations. Part nod, part shake, it generally means 'yes' or 'I understand', but can also stand for 'thank you' or an all-purpose acknowledgement.

DRESS CODES

Although it is keen to open itself up to tourists, Kerala is a traditional state, and its citizens have not been exposed to the liberal Western practices that have become everyday for Goans. Outside the more touristy resorts, local people would be taken aback if a visitor stripped down to their swimwear. You're unlikely to meet any hostility – Keralans are too friendly for that – but a slightly more modest attitude to attire is appreciated. For obvious reasons, topless sunbathing is a no-no. In religious buildings, modest dress is even more of a must. In mosques, this means women covering their heads, arms and legs. Take your shoes off (or at least offer to) before entering a home or place of worship.

ELECTRICITY

India's voltage system is 220–240 V. Electrical sockets tend to be of the European, two-pin kind, but some places have fitted British three-pin sockets too. The better hotels have adaptors on hand. If you're travelling with US or Canadian appliances, bring a transformer. Kerala's electricity supply can be erratic, and you may experience power cuts.

EMERGENCIES

If you're taken ill and need treatment the first port of call should be your hotel or driver, if you have one, who can advise you where to seek help. The standard of medical facilities is variable in India; in general, your

EMERGENCY NUMBERS
Police 100, 112
Fire 101
Ambulance 102

chances of finding a more professional, well-equipped clinic improve with the size of the town. The most highly rated medical facilities in the major towns are listed below. A more extensive list can be found at:
🌐 www.hospitalskerala.com

Kerala Institute of Medical Sciences 🅰 Anayara, Trivandrum
📞 (0471) 407 1000 🌐 www.kimskerala.com

Lakeshore Hospital 🅰 NH 47 Bypass, Maradu, Nettor, Kochi
📞 (0484) 270 1032 🌐 www.lakeshorehospital.com

Kerala's police are often helpful and friendly to tourists. However, should you have to file a report, expect the procedure to be somewhat laborious.

EMBASSIES
There are no embassies in Kerala, the nearest ports of call being either Chennai, over on the east coast, or Mumbai or Bangalore to the north.
British Deputy High Commission 🅰 20 Anderson Road, Chennai
📞 (044) 4219 2151 📠 (044) 4219 2322 🌐 http:ukinindia.fco.gov.uk
📧 bdhcchen@airtelmail.in
Honorary Consul of Ireland 🅰 c/o Biocon Limited, 20th KM Hosur Road, Bangalore 📞 (080) 2808 2006 📠 (080) 2852 1660 🌐 www.dfa.ie
📧 kiran.mazumdar@bioconindia.com
US Consulate General 🅰 Gemini Circle, Chennai 📞 (044) 2857 4000
📠 (044) 2811 2020 🌐 http://chennai.usconsulate.gov
📧 chennaics@state.gov
Consulate of Canada 🅰 18 (Old 24), third floor YAFA Tower, Khader Nawaz Khan Road, Nungambakkam, Chennai 📞 (044) 2833 0888 📠 (044) 4215 9393 🌐 www.canadainternational.gc.ca 📧 cheni@gocindia.org

GETTING AROUND

Auto-rickshaw

The classic Indian form of transport is the auto-rickshaw or *tuktuk*, a three-wheeler, motorised cart. This must be experienced at least once during your time in Kerala. Though not as cheap as public transport, it is still inexpensive (especially if you bargain hard), usually about half the price of the equivalent taxi ride. Bear in mind that the poor condition of the roads can result in a very bumpy ride.

Bus

If you're on a tight budget and are not of a particularly sensitive disposition, Kerala's extensive bus network is another good way to travel the state. Buses go fairly frequently between the towns, and fares – you typically pay the driver once on board – are unbelievably cheap. The downside is the lack of comfort. State buses can get unpleasantly cramped, and you may have to stand or sit squashed against your fellow passengers. There is no glass in the windows, which can be a problem when it rains. The suspension – or seeming total lack thereof – will ensure a lively journey. Express buses between the major hubs can be a little more luxurious, often with air conditioning (and windows). ⓦ www.keralartc.com

Car Hire

India has some of the worst driving conditions in the world, and Kerala is no exception. Potholed roads, rogue animals and the cavalier attitudes of other drivers to such niceties as indicating and checking for oncoming traffic combine to create road-based chaos. Only the very brave tourist would consider self-drive, and the options for that are consequently very limited. A more popular method is to rent a car with a driver. The same man can stay with you for the duration of your travels, sleeping either in the car or at cheap flophouses. This option gives you the assurance that your baggage is safe and avoids having to deal with new drivers for different legs. It's equally possible to do some legs of your journey by taxi, alternating with public transport. Most drivers are prepared to negotiate a day rate, or give a quote for your proposed journey.

Train

India's train journeys are the stuff of legend. More comfortable than the bus, it can still sometimes be difficult to get a seat, and the reservation system is fiendishly unfathomable to the outsider. But they represent great value for money, afford an opportunity to get chatting to the local people and also scythe through some superlative scenery, particularly in the north of the state where the train glides alongside pristine beaches unknown to most tourists.

HEALTH, SAFETY AND CRIME

Kerala is subject to the same health risks as the rest of India, chiefly: dodgy food and water, hot sun, stray animals and demented traffic. Start your trip with simple, mild food, as tucking straight into the spicy stuff can be a one-way ticket to the dreaded Delhi belly. Never drink the tap water, avoid salad and ice unless you're in an upmarket hotel or restaurant, eat piping-hot, cooked food and make sure you peel fruit. Standard sun protection advice applies: use high-factor sun cream, even when it's cloudy; stay out of the sun in the hottest part of the day; keep well hydrated. Kerala is a low-risk area for malaria but it's still worth using mosquito repellent and a net, coils or spray if you're not in a well-sealed, air-conditioned room. Avoid approaching stray animals (monkeys may look cute but can turn aggressive).

The more professional clinics that cater for tourists will have higher standards, but will be correspondingly more expensive. Some of the better medical facilities are listed in the Emergencies section.

Crime levels are relatively low in Kerala, but of course any place where 'rich' Westerners are in close proximity with the very poor creates temptation and opportunity for the criminally minded. Be as safety conscious as you would in any foreign city. Don't advertise your valuables and keep a close eye on your possessions and pockets in any crowded place, particularly on public transport. While Kerala is not an obvious target for terrorism, India does have sectarian tensions. It's best to avoid

political demonstrations and other potential flashpoints. Keralan police wear easily recognisable khaki uniforms and, despite an unenviable reputation for corruption, generally go to great lengths to help tourists.

MEDIA

Because English is so widely spoken in India, there will be no shortage of news if you wish to keep up to date. Kerala's own newspapers are in the state language of Malayalam, but the *Malayala Manorama* does have an online version in English. Respected national *The Hindu* has a regional edition, and you can also find the *Indian Express* and a clutch of English-language magazines.

There's plenty of English-language content on television, both through Indian channels like Star TV and the cable staples of BBC World, CNN, MTV and the like. Some radio stations also broadcast in English.

Malayala Manorama Ⓦ www.manoramaonline.com

The Hindu Ⓦ www.hinduonnet.com

Indian Express Ⓦ www.indianexpress.com

OPENING HOURS

Offices are open from 09.30 to 17.30 or 18.00 Monday to Friday, banks from 10.00 to 14.00 on weekdays and until noon on Saturday. Post offices also open at 10.00 and close their doors on weekdays between 16.30 and 18.30, depending on their size, and at noon or 16.30 on Saturday. Shops trade from about 10.00 to 18.00 or 19.00; few do Sundays. Restaurants tend to be all-day affairs, starting the breakfast shift around 08.00 and running through until 22.00 or thereabouts. There are no real hard and fast rules for attractions, although not much would be open after 17.00 or 18.00, and some are closed on Mondays.

RELIGION

Just over half of Keralans are Hindus. Almost a quarter are Muslims, and slightly under a fifth are Christians, most of whom are Syrian Orthodox. Sikhs, Jains, Buddhists and Jews make up the rest. For the most part, the groups rub along quite well together.

SMOKING

Kerala has now enacted tough anti-smoking legislation, prohibiting lighting up in all public places, which technically includes the street. Flouting the law can mean a fine or even prison, although in practice people can and do find ways to sneak a crafty cigarette. Hotels usually set aside a small, outdoor area for their nicotine-consuming guests, but in restaurants smokers may have to pop outside and find a hidden spot.

TIME DIFFERENCES

Kerala is 5.5 hours ahead of GMT, 4.5 ahead of most of mainland Europe. It is 10.5 ahead of EST and 13.5 ahead of PST, 5.5 hours behind Sydney and 7.5 behind Auckland. India doesn't have daylight saving, so these times may vary by an hour.

TIPPING

Small tips are appreciated in Kerala, where wages are low by Western standards. In a restaurant you could leave ten per cent of the bill. Some of the more upmarket hotels, recognising many visitors' squeamishness about this area, may include a service charge of around that amount, or encourage satisfied customers to leave some cash in an envelope to be disbursed evenly, rather than to tip an individual staff member. Hotel employees who've struggled under the weight of your luggage and drivers who've been particularly helpful or friendly also welcome a small consideration.

TOILETS

While high-end hotels will have the pristine conveniences you'd expect in any such establishment anywhere in the world, further downmarket lavatorial standards can be hit and miss. Most businesses that cater for tourists have worked out that they like to sit down on the loo and have access to toilet paper. However, off the beaten track you are likely to be confronted with the dreaded squat toilet. Most Indians don't use toilet paper and it is often absent – carry a supply of tissues with you at all times. On the positive side, facilities, though basic, are usually fairly clean.

TRAVELLERS WITH DISABILITIES

India is still a developing country, and disabled rights are unfortunately not afforded the importance they are elsewhere. Kerala is no picnic to get around if your mobility or sight is impaired. Pavements – when such a luxury exists – are often narrow and uneven, and traffic chaotic. Crossing busy Keralan roads can be daunting even for the able-bodied. Away from the best hotels, there is precious little in the way of wheelchair access. On the plus side, Keralans tend to be as obliging as possible to tourists, and the general cheapness of travel makes staying in specially adapted accommodation and hiring a car and driver, a guide or even bringing a travel companion from home (some disabled groups may be able to help you link up with someone) more affordable. You could also consider booking through a specialised travel agency, which will have a better understanding of your needs. The following organisations offer various degrees of advice to travellers with disabilities:

The **Royal Association for Disability and Rehabilitation** does not run an advice service for individuals, but there is some general information on travel, and its website has a section on the news bulletin board on which the editor posts details of overseas travel services. @ 12 City Forum, 250 City Road, London, EC1V 8AF ☎ (020) 7250 3222 📠 (020) 7250 0212 🌐 www.radar.org.uk ✉ radar@radar.org.uk

Tourism for All provides some helpful advice and information on overseas travel. @ c/o Vitalise, Shap Road Industrial Estate, Shap Road, Kendal, Cumbria, LA9 6NZ ☎ 0845 124 9971 📠 01539 735567 ✉ info@tourismforall.org.uk

ACKNOWLEDGEMENTS

The publishers would like to thank the following for providing their copyright photographs for this book: Getty Images page 31; Photoshot/World Pictures page 19; Pictures Colour Library page 38; Vasile Szakacs pages 5, 9, 10, 13, 16, 20, 24, 27, 28, 36, 42, 44, 46, 49, 51, 56, 59, 61, 63, 65, 67, 71, 73, 75, 77, 78, 80, 81, 83, 85, 88, 91, 93, 95, 101, 102, 105, 109, 115

Project editor: Catherine Burch
Layout: Paul Queripel
Proofreader: Nick Newton
Indexer: Karolin Thomas

Send your thoughts to
books@thomascook.com

- Found a beach bar, peaceful stretch of sand or must-see sight that we don't feature?

- Like to tip us off about any information that needs a little updating?

- Want to tell us what you love about this handy little guidebook and more importantly how we can make it even handier?

Then here's your chance to tell all! Send us ideas, discoveries and recommendations today and then look out for your valuable input in the next edition of this title.

Send an email to the above address or write to:
pocket guides Series Editor, Thomas Cook Publishing, PO Box 227, Coningsby Road, Peterborough PE3 8SB, UK

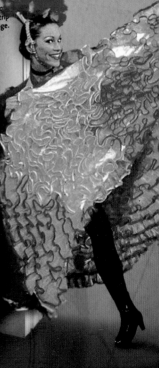

shed
nds,
avel.

s our
crets
orld,
th of
avel

yo
trip
tage.

Thomas Cook **pocket** guides

PARIS

Your travelling companion since 1873

Thomas Cook